France's
Vietnam
Policy

Contributions in Political Science
Series Editor: Bernard K. Johnpoll

American Democratic Theory: Pluralism and Its Critics
William Alton Kelso

International Terrorism in the Contemporary World
Marius H. Livingston, with Lee Bruce Kress and Marie G. Wanek, editors

Doves and Diplomats: Foreign Offices and Peace Movements in Europe and America in the Twentieth Century
Solomon Wank, editor

Believing Skeptics: American Political Intellectuals, 1945-1964
Robert Booth Fowler

Locke, Rousseau, and the Idea of Consent: An Inquiry into the Liberal–Democratic Theory of Political Obligation
Jules Steinberg

Judicial Craftsmanship or Fiat?: Direct Overturn by the United States Supreme Court
Howard Ball

The Tragedy of Chile
Robert J. Alexander

The New Left in France: The Unified Socialist Party
Charles Hauss

The Communist Parties of Western Europe: A Comparative Study
R. Neal Tannahill

France's Vietnam Policy

A STUDY IN FRENCH-AMERICAN RELATIONS

Marianna P. Sullivan

GREENWOOD PRESS

Contributions in
Political Science, Number 12

WESPORT, CONNECTICUT • LONDON, ENGLAND

Library of Congress Cataloging in Publication Data

Sullivan, Marianna P
    France's Vietnam policy.

    (Contributions in political science; no. 12
ISSN 0147-1066)
    Bibliography: p.
    Includes index.
    1. Vietnamese Conflict, 1961-1975—France.
2. France—Foreign relations—United States. 3. United
States—Foreign relations—France. I. Title.
II. Series.
DS558.6.F8S93   959.704'3344   77-94749
ISBN 0-313-20317-2

Portions of "France's Policy toward the Second Indochina
War" by Marianna P. Sullivan, in Gene T. Hsiao, ed., *The
Role of External Powers in the Indochina Crisis* (Edwardsville, Illinois: Southern Illinois University, 1973), pp. 42-64,
reprinted by permission.

Library of Congress Catalog Card Number: 77-94749
ISBN: 0-313-20317-2
ISSN: 0147-1066

First published in 1978

Greenwood Press, Inc.
51 Riverside Avenue, Westport, Connecticut 06880

Printed in the United States of America

10 9 8 7 6 5 4 3 2 1

To Michael

Contents

Acknowledgments

Many people have aided me in one way or another regarding the preparation of this volume and I thank them all. I am particularly indebted to those individuals who discussed with me their involvement in France's Vietnam policy, especially Jean Sainteny, former French delegate to Hanoi who spoke with me on three occasions and Etienne Manac'h who kindly met with me in 1972 while on a brief vacation in France from his duties as ambassador to Peking. Both of these gentlemen shared with me the views and recollections that were products of their personal experiences in France and Asia. Their conversations with me not only yielded useful information but also made the events we discussed come alive.

The research and writing of this volume were facilitated by two grants of released time from the Trenton State College Faculty Research Committee. I thank the committee members and the college officials under whose administration the funding for research time was made available: President Clayton R. Brower, Vice-President Gordon I. Goewey, and Dean Wade C. Curry. Also deserving of my thanks are Melvin Sykes, who provided research assistance, Sueann Rosen, who typed the manuscript, and Madame Monique Polgar of the French Embassy's Press and Information Division in New York. Madame Polgar's continuing assistance in securing documentary materials is most appreciated.

Early in my life I learned the value of intellectual enterprises from my parents, John J. Pulaski and the late Mary K. Pulaski. I thank them both. More recently, my son Jeremy has helped by his philosophic acceptance of my daily departures to "bring home the bacons." When he learns to read, he will find here my acknowledgment of his sacrifices.

Finally, my biggest debt is to my husband, Dr. Michael J. Sullivan III, who is a constant source of personal and professional encouragement. With respect to this volume, my husband and colleague was patient and supportive but not uncritical. This book is dedicated to him.

Introduction

The critical French reaction to American involvement in Vietnam from
1963 to 1973 was often regarded by American policy makers as routine
Gaullist anti-Americanism. A more complex assessment reveals that
France's posture toward the Vietnam war was the result of many factors,
including, but not limited to, Charles de Gaulle's attitude toward the
United States. An examination of the variety of circumstances that
determined French policy toward the American-Vietnamese war indicates the following: France and the United States had quarreled over
their respective roles in Vietnam since World War II; this quarrel reflected
the basic tension between the two allies during a period of French decline and American ascendance; and France's Vietnam policy from 1963
to 1973 was a dynamic response to changing Vietnamese circumstances
and evolving French-American relations.

   Thus, France's policy toward what has been called the "second Indochina war" may be viewed in terms of three types of factors: relational,
historical, and situational. The relational factors are so-called because
they indicate the relationship between the different areas of the Fifth
Republic's foreign policy. Chiefly, France's posture on Vietnam reflected
de Gaulle's major themes: independence from United States leadership
in Europe and pursuit of France's global role. The latter has not been
examined by scholars as fully as his European and NATO policies. These

relational factors are discussed in Part I, Chapter 1. In particular, attention is called to the tension between France and the United States which formed a central theme in de Gaulle's foreign policy as well as that of his predecessors in the Fourth Republic. De Gaulle expressed concern over America's postwar dominance in contexts where the issue of French dependence on the United States could be joined, such as NATO, and in areas that were peripheral to French-American relations, such as Vietnam.

Furthermore, Chapter 1 discusses the other priorities in Gaullist foreign policy: European and global affairs. De Gaulle's first public comment on Vietnam on August 29, 1963, coincided with his increased emphasis on non-European areas. While Europe remained his main focus, he sought to exercise a global role based partially on France's relations with less developed countries; this emphasis became possible after France's reputation in the Third World was cleansed by the 1962 Algerian settlement.

Parallels can be drawn between de Gaulle's Asian and European policies—chiefly, his encouragement of conditions of fluidity which would lessen France's dependence on the United States and increase its room for maneuver. De Gaulle's position on Vietnam reflected this aim as well as his inclination to issue grand pronouncements on international events.

The historical determinants of France's attitude toward the United States role in Vietnam during the 1960s are considered in Part II, Chapters 2 and 3. The former examines the quarrels between the two countries over Indochina during the period immediately following World War II when the French began their futile struggle to retain control there. United States policy was sometimes at cross-purposes with this French aim. Although de Gaulle was on the sidelines while all of this took place, he could not fail to note the spectacle of France's American ally equating its own interests with those of France in an area of primary French concern. Moreover, France's inability to defeat the forces of national liberation (repeated eight years later in Algeria) deeply impressed him and later influenced his attitude toward American involvement in Vietnam.

The degree to which de Gaulle's analysis of Vietnamese affairs varied from that of the United States during the 1960s is discussed in Chapter 3. The late French president sincerely believed that the issues in Vietnam were local and that no amount of military power could resolve them. Moreover, his ideas about Vietnam were shared by political and public opinion in France. These differing French-American perspectives were

revealed in two instances prior to the escalation of American involvement in Vietnam: during the Laotian crises of 1960-62 and during events
in Saigon culminating in the assassination of Ngo Dinh Diem in 1963.

The situational factors or the shifting circumstances in Southeast Asia
to which French policy reacted are reviewed in Part III, Chapters 4 and
5. The former discusses French policy during the escalatory period of
1965-68. After his initial public comment about Vietnam in 1963, and
as the war and United States participation in it expanded, de Gaulle was
harshly critical of American policy in Vietnam. Naturally, the United
States resented the content and public nature of this criticism so that
de Gaulle's Vietnam stance increased the disharmony that characterized
French-American relations during this period.

The Vietnam war provided de Gaulle with an opportunity to dissociate France from American actions; nevertheless, French policy in this
and other areas was subject to severe limitations. First, France's concern
for Vietnam and its expertise in Vietnamese affairs could not be applied
to a situation dominated by overwhelming American power. Free and
willing to criticize, de Gaulle was well aware that he could not alter American actions. Second, the tone and content of de Gaulle's pronouncements
regarding American policy in Vietnam were so familiar that they were
easily dismissed in Washington as new variations on a very old theme.
Furthermore, de Gaulle preferred drama to persuasion. It did not suit his
political style to present his arguments against United States policy in
Vietnam in private or in conjunction with other interested parties. Instead, he launched a unilateral public attack on American policy in
Southeast Asia. It is doubtful that a more subtle approach would have
altered United States policy, but de Gaulle's chosen course sacrificed the
benefits other alternatives might have offered. Third, any potential French
involvement in attempts to negotiate a solution in Vietnam was contin-
gent upon conditions that France was powerless to influence. In Vietnam
and elsewhere, the French role depended upon the attitudes of various
interested parties, especially the United States.

France's position toward the Vietnam war altered drastically in the
period of declining American involvement in Vietnam and the ongoing
Paris peace talks. Greater sympathy with the American position as United
States troops left Southeast Asia—and French-American relations improved
more generally—combined with French hopes for a role in the peace settlement and afterwards in Vietnam produced a more neutral French posture.

However, limits on French effectiveness, such as those mentioned earlier, persisted. France's Vietnam policy as the 1973 agreement evolved is discussed in Chapter 5.

Finally, the "Conclusion" unites the themes of all three parts to provide an assessment of France's Vietnam policy as a product of relational, historical, and situational factors. The Vietnam war is a case study that illustrates some themes of the Fifth Republic's foreign policy, especially its continuing preoccupation with the French-American relationship. In Vietnam and elsewhere, de Gaulle expressed aggravation with the United States which was shared in some degree by his predecessors. Moreover, the limits on French-American cooperation that have persisted under de Gaulle's successors cannot be ignored. Finally, the long period of French-American discord regarding Vietnam is a significant element in the history of America's longest and most controversial war.

A word on sources is in order. In addition to secondary sources, such as books and articles on French foreign policy, primary sources were employed in the form of government documents, eyewitness newspaper accounts, memoirs, and interviews. Since there are few secondary sources that discuss France's global policy in general and its Vietnam position in particular, primary sources were used extensively in every chapter except Chapter 1, which outlines France's NATO and European policies. Several sources were of particular importance. First, the memoirs of Jean Sainteny, the French official initially in charge of reasserting control over Indochina in 1945, were invaluable. Curiously, these have never been translated into English nor used extensively by American scholars exploring the origins of the Vietnam war.

Second, the Defense Department study popularly known as the "Pentagon Papers" provides clear illustrations of the divergence between French and American policy in Southeast Asia since 1945. Attention has previously focused on those portions of the Pentagon study that pertain to events in the 1960s while its inclusive account of the earlier period was initially ignored; the value of these earlier volumes in tracing the origins of United States involvement should be apparent.

Third, the resources available at the John F. Kennedy Library were utilized to examine the 1961-63 period. These include oral history interviews with American officials, such as Ambassador to Laos Winthrop Brown and Ambassador to South Vietnam Henry Cabot Lodge, as well as those documents concerning Vietnam from the National Security Council's files, some of which have been recently declassified.

Finally, over sixty interviews with various French, American, and Vietnamese respondents, most of whom are former or current officials, provide a unique perspective on the entire postwar period of disharmony between France and the United States over Vietnam. Most of these interviews were conducted in Paris during the summers of 1972 and 1973; they lasted an average of sixty minutes each. The comments of such former and present French officials as Jean Sainteny, Jean Chauvel (ambassador to the 1954 and 1961-62 Geneva conferences), Roger Lalouette (ambassador to Saigon, 1963), Etienne Manac'h (ambassador to Peking 1969-75), and Maurice Schumann (former foreign minister) were rich in detail and anecdote.

Naturally the use of oral sources imposes a special burden on the researcher. Evaluation of the information conveyed is complicated by the immediacy of the interview process and the paucity of written sources against which the respondent's account can be compared. Nevertheless, regardless of its pitfalls, interviewing is often the only method of ascertaining the perspective of officials who have not written extensively on sensitive events. Interviews are especially essential to any analysis of recent events; without them the pages that follow would not be complete.

Part I | RELATIONAL FACTORS

Chapter 1

Gaullism Reexamined

GAULLISM AND FOREIGN AFFAIRS

France's attitude toward American policy in Vietnam during the ten years of major American involvement, 1963-73, was a function of the historic discord between France and the United States over Indochina, of the evolving situation in Vietnam, and of Charles de Gaulle's foreign policy. History formed the precedent for the Fifth Republic's Vietnam policy in two ways: it was the source of both French claims to expertise regarding Indochina and their skepticism of United States actions there. The situational aspects set the limits on the exercise of French policy by de Gaulle and by his successor as president of the Fifth Republic, Georges Pompidou. However, it was Charles de Gaulle who determined the primacy of foreign policy in the Fifth Republic and enunciated its major themes. Thus, an examination of de Gaulle's goals and priorities is in order so that the Vietnam case can be viewed in context and its wider importance to an understanding of French foreign policy can be appreciated.

Charles de Gaulle's foreign policy has not suffered for lack of analysis by scholars who have tended to regard him either as lion or as pygmy. To some he is a hero of mythic quality who rescued French pride in 1940, French institutions in 1958, and French integrity in 1962. They view these accomplishments—acting as the voice of Free France, becoming the first leader of the Fifth Republic, and giving Algeria independence— as milestones in recent French history. Others cannot contemplate Charles de Gaulle's foreign policy without emphasizing the limits that surrounded it. To them, de Gaulle's attempt to live beyond France's means was an impossible dream. Both of these extreme views betray a preoccupation with de Gaulle himself. To both critics and admirers de Gaulle was the moving force behind French foreign policy while he served as president of the Fifth Republic from 1958 to 1969.

Therefore, analysis of France's Vietnam policy during the American involvement (1963-73) must begin with a brief examination of de Gaulle's foreign policy. It is important to identify his perceptions of international affairs and his main objectives indicating through selected examples how he sought to implement them. Finally, it is necessary to indicate the relevance of the Vietnam situation to de Gaulle's foreign policy themes so as to demonstrate that Vietnam, though a peripheral area of French policy during the 1960s, was typical of the style and substance of the Gaullist approach to foreign affairs.

De Gaulle was guided in his choice of goals and tactics by his political philosophy and by his perception of the limits and possibilities presented by the international system during the 1960s.[1] His own philosophy emphasized the role of great powers and great men in public affairs. He argued repeatedly that France was destined to be a great power in spite of the frail leadership that sometimes led her out of the front rank. Clearly, he meant to provide leadership of another kind; de Gaulle enunciated his vision of France's future by dominating the areas of foreign and defense policy with decisions often made by his own staff at the Elysée Palace instead of at the foreign and defense ministries. His irrational notion of France's historic role was complemented by his belief in the primacy of the nation-state in international affairs. He argued that the nation-state was historically the legitimate actor internationally and that "nuclear logic," the necessity in a nuclear age for each state to provide for its own defense, reinforced the classic state system. Thus, insofar as the character of nuclear war drew into question the commitment of one nation to die for another, de Gaulle believed that sovereignty was reinforced by the nuclear age; in matters of self-defense he considered France's right to determine its fate equal to the challenge of American nuclear superiority. Due to their destructive capacity which lends doubt about their use, nuclear weapons cannot be translated directly into political influence. Thus, de Gaulle questioned the United States commitment to defend France with American nuclear weapons and resisted the United States efforts to translate its protective promise into influence over France's foreign policy.

Politics, domestic or international, were for de Gaulle a struggle in which the strong prevailed. While he admitted the bipolar nature of international politics after 1945, he accepted with reluctance any restrictions on France's freedom of action which might stem from bipolarity. Instead, he sought to resist domination by either the United States or the Soviet Union. Since he viewed ideologies as transitory, he believed that the construction of international politics in the 1950s along bipolar ideological lines was artificial. In his view, Russian national interest rather than Marxism-Leninism was the determinant of Soviet foreign policy, and he became the first Western leader to visit Moscow after World War II; his policy of rapprochement with Russia and Eastern Europe preceded President Lyndon Johnson's bridge-building and Chancellor Willy Brandt's Ostpolitik. His attempt to facilitate the breakup of the blocs also entailed extending recognition to mainland China in 1964.

A seminal event in postwar international politics, according to de Gaulle, was the Cuban missile crisis of 1962. Although the French proudly point out that France was the first country to rally to President Kennedy's support in his face-off with the Russians, de Gaulle drew two conclusions from the situation: first, in an ultimate crisis, the United States confronted the Soviet Union with their respective allies' fate determined by duopolistic patterns; and, second, both powers recoiled from the use of nuclear weapons, thereby reducing the likelihood of future nuclear war. De Gaulle further reasoned that if nuclear weapons were not to be used, another basis for bipolarity was rendered inoperative. By this reasoning, the Cuban missile crisis ushered in the era of détente that began with the 1963 Partial Test-ban Treaty, and it also marked the end of bipolarity because the lessened threat of war freed the superpowers' allies from having to support them unequivocally.[2] Thus, after 1962, France's capacity for freedom of action was enhanced.

During the latter half of the 1960s de Gaulle perceived the world as unifocal: he believed that international politics was dominated by the United States. Thus his rejection of the two hegemonies was replaced by his condemnation of a singular threat to French independence emanating from the United States. France's retreat from a foreign policy harmonized with that of the United States led, in 1967, to adoption of the strategy of *la défense tous-azimuts* (defense in all directions), which proclaimed

France ready to meet an attack from the West as well as from the East. This doctrine was abandoned one year later when the Czechoslovakian invasion reinstated the cold war battle lines.

It was against a background of modified bipolarity that de Gaulle pursued his four objectives:

1. Resolution of the Algerian Problem
2. Greater Influence vis-à-vis the United States
3. Leadership in Europe
4. A Global Role

There is no question about the primacy of foreign policy for Charles de Gaulle. However, during the first four years of his presidency he was preoccupied with what the French regarded as a domestic issue—the independence movement in Algeria. Resolution of the Algerian question was essential both in order to solidify the institutions of the Fifth Republic—indeed, the Algerian revolt had destroyed the Fifth Republic's predecessor—but also in order to pursue more vigorously the global role that de Gaulle sought for France. He could not hope to increase French influence, especially among Third World nations, while the Algerian problem remained unsolved. His own recognition of the inevitability of decolonization after World War II was clear in his policy toward French colonies in Africa south of the Sahara all of which had achieved independence by 1960.

De Gaulle's handling of the Algerian situation was a remarkable display of practical politics. He concluded that a military solution was not possible and concentrated his efforts on a settlement least offensive to French interests and in accord with the political realities. He approached this objective with the support of most Frenchmen because his equivocal statements between 1958 and 1961 were interpreted favorably by opinion on both sides of the issue. Whether his equivocation was the result of his own indecision matters less than its effect of muting all sectors of French opinion and massing the majority on the side of an independent Algeria.[3] Furthermore, although he maintained a facade of continuity, de Gaulle wisely retreated from positions that became untenable. In January 1960, he declared his refusal to negotiate with the Algerian National Liberation Front (FLN), and in June 1960, he reversed this posture; although at first he agreed only to bargain with groups including the FLN, he ultimately accepted that group as his sole negotiating partner.

After the Evian accords of 1962 granted Algerian independence, de Gaulle was determined to redeem France's image in the Third World by inaugurating a policy of cooperation with Algeria. He directed a large percentage of his country's economic aid program to Algeria, acquiesced in the confiscation of French property in violation of the Evian accords, accepted agreements heavily favoring the host country for the right to exploit its oil resources—all this without interruption for the benefit of two Algerian regimes which professed to follow a "socialist" foreign policy. France's dividends from this huge investment extended beyond the sphere of bilateral relations with Algeria. Rather, the *raison d'être* of de Gaulle's Algerian policy was the example of France, the ex-colonizer, expiating a debt to a former colony and reestablishing its credentials to act as friend to the less developed.[4]

GREATER INFLUENCE VIS-A-VIS THE UNITED STATES

HISTORIC PRECEDENTS

Sharing de Gaulle's attention with the Algerian question was the issue of France's relationship with the United States. His desire to increase French influence vis-à-vis its major ally brought him into conflict with American policy at the outset of his presidency. Moreover, de Gaulle's anti-Americanism was not without historic precedent. Like de Gaulle, the leaders of the Fourth Republic (1946-58) sought to maintain France's global role in some form, and they expressed deep resentment of American influence on French affairs.[5] Their desire for political prestige and for influence over France's major ally led the Fourth Republic's leaders in 1956 to begin development of France's nuclear capacity. The purpose of the nuclear force was the same in their minds as in de Gaulle's: to secure for France status comparable with that of Great Britain, whose special relationship with the United States aroused their jealousy.[6]

Indeed, France's foreign policy since World War II has revolved around its relations with the United States. The physical effects of defeat and occupation were alleviated after France was liberated by American soldiers and reconstructed with Marshall Plan aid, but the psychological burdens persisted. Moreover, France's reduced status was more difficult to bear because of its dependence on the United States. The subordination of French defense policy to that of the United States when the latter's responsibilities expanded globally as those of France contracted was not easily tolerated by a nation that regarded itself as a historically great power.

American officials sometimes seemed unsympathetic to the problems created by France's adjustment to its postwar status and insensitive to the frustrations experienced by France's leaders. In Europe, the United States accompanied its massive economic and military assistance with support for European unity that appeared over-zealous to the French. Resentment of American pressure in favor of the proposed European Defense Community contributed to the latter's defeat in 1954. On colonial matters the French viewed as ambiguous American policy toward France's quest to retain control over Indochina and Algeria. Instead of solidarity behind French policy, the United States extended conditional support, which complicated the efforts of beleaguered French governments to pursue a coherent and effective course.

France's dissatisfaction with United States policy during its colonial war in Indochina (1946-54) was a particularly good example of American policy, which the Fourth Republic's leaders viewed as contrary to their interests. The United States, in keeping with its Asian policy at the time, had made no effort to assist the French when the Japanese moved against Indochina in 1939-40 nor to hasten the reassertion of French control in 1945. The interruption of the independent exercise of French sovereignty in Indochina had the same effect that similar circumstances had for the Dutch in Indonesia, namely, giving valuable momentum to the indigenous movement for political independence.

United States policy toward Indochina in the closing months of World War II vacillated between Roosevelt's desire to grant the French colonies independence or United Nations trusteeship status and his commitment to the Free French that the *status quo ante* would obtain in France's colonies. Finally, in April 1945, United States policy clearly favored (though without much enthusiasm) the return of Indochina to France. This belated support did not prevent the outbreak of hostilities between French and Vietnamese forces in December 1946. In April 1950, two months before the Korean War began, President Truman promised to support France against the Viet Minh. From 1950 to 1954, American financial support for the French war effort in Indochina was considerable and was accompanied by the unsolicited and unwelcome advice that France grant the Vietnamese complete independence under a pro-Western government. At the 1954 Geneva conference, which arranged terms for the French withdrawal from Indochina, the two allies did not agree on goals or tactics and the United States expressed its distaste for the accords

France had concluded by refusing to assent to them and subsequently ignoring their provisions. The events of 1945 to 1954 are discussed in detail in Chapter 2. They comprise a particularly bitter episode in French-American relations that historically preceded the disagreement between the two allies over Vietnam in the 1960s.

Furthermore, French-American discord over Indochina in the late 1940s and the 1950s was indicative of French-American relations more generally. United States policy toward the French colonial struggle in Southeast Asia aroused strong resentment among the French who believed that the United States acted in violation of France's interests. In fact, de Gaulle later expressed his suspicion that the United States had always intended to replace France in Indochina. United States policy in Asia was justified in terms of cold war responses, and the French themselves were adept at exploiting the anti-Communist argument to gain United States support for their war in Indochina. However, the cold war imperatives that united the allies in a common cause did not, in France's view, justify a subjection of France's foreign policy to that of the United States. On the contrary, as de Gaulle later argued, in areas where France had particular interests, such as Indochina or Algeria, American policy should follow France's lead. American leaders did not share this view. Consequently, the theme of resentment of the United States, or anti-Americanism, has permeated France's foreign policy since 1945.

UNIQUE CIRCUMSTANCES

In spite of these historical precedents, de Gaulle's approach to French-American relations during the 1960s was unique in several ways. Domestically, the Fourth Republic proved unstable; successive cabinets were constrained by the temporary nature of their mandate which imposed a course of moderation and compromise rather than one of boldness and innovation.[7] This was particularly true with respect to Indochina from 1946 to 1954, when policy became static and lost direction. In contrast, de Gaulle inaugurated a period of stability in French politics that enabled him to assert a sense of national self-possession and a widespread disillusionment with American leadership that were deeply felt in postwar France. This stability persists to the present. The institutions that Michel Debré created for the Fifth Republic according to de Gaulle's specifications equipped the French executive with the authority to govern effectively. De Gaulle's personal charisma was the necessary complement to the office, and his tenure as its first occupant gave the institutions their start. In fact, de Gaulle was fond of identifying himself with order and threatening, in the manner of Louis XIV, that his departure would bring chaos. During the first years of the Fifth Republic this argument was convincing to the French and de Gaulle's popularity remained high. In these circumstances and unlike his predecessors, de Gaulle enjoyed tremendous support in France for his foreign policy. Only during the last years of his presidency did de Gaulle lose the support of the French. Their rejection of him in the referendum of March 1969 affirmed their faith in the institutions of the Fifth Republic without de Gaulle.

Internationally, the circumstances in the 1960s were suited to a reassertion of France's global role and, in particular, to de Gaulle's criticism of the United States. Its economic and political recovery complete, Europe could claim greater influence, and France, under de Gaulle, was in a unique position to assert this claim; neither Britain nor West Germany was sufficiently independent of the United States to make a similar assertion. Furthermore, de Gaulle's critique of United States policy became more virulent as America's supreme global status began to decline. American involvement in Vietnam marked the end of her certain leadership of global affairs and introduced doubts about American policy externally as well as within the United States itself. In such circumstances, de Gaulle's criticism of United States policy in general and of Vietnam in particular seemed appropriate.

Indeed, the Vietnam issue was explicitly linked in de Gaulle's mind with the fundamental question he posed concerning French-American relations, namely, to what extent can France allow the United States to determine its policy in the vital area of defense. De Gaulle's answer was to reserve France's judgment on most matters, thereby assuming in effect the stance of a "neutral."[8]

INDEPENDENCE IN NATO

De Gaulle's posture within and without NATO can be linked to a single article of faith—independence. For him, independence was both a characteristic of policy making and a policy objective; it was a tactic as well as a goal. Some observers have judged de Gaulle's policy anachronistic because of its emphasis on the prerogatives of the nation-state. Indeed, following nearly a decade of progress toward European unity (1949-57) and thus of movement beyond the nation-state, de Gaulle's emphasis on French independence seemed outmoded. It is perhaps more understandable when viewed in terms of the decade after de Gaulle's retirement: since 1969 the issues he raised in the context of the Atlantic Alliance persist. That is, Europeans accuse the United States of failing to consult its allies and of neglecting to resolve alliance conflicts. Thus, in retrospect de Gaulle's questions about the compatibility of alliance interests no longer seem as shocking as they did in the 1960s.

Nevertheless, de Gaulle's Atlantic policy upset United States leaders because it challenged their cherished assumptions about American leadership of a unified Western alliance. Obsessed with the pursuit of an independent French foreign policy, de Gaulle argued that France's actions everywhere and, in particular, its relations with its allies should reflect the freedom of action inherent in a sovereign power. In fact, he challenged the concept of permanent alliances; according to his philosophy, states always pursue their national interest *as they define it,* thereby creating difficulties for alliance agreements that compromise future freedom of action. He believed that alliances are formed essentially to augment a nation's powers to defend itself against a specific threat, and alliance commitments should be honored in accord with changing perceptions of national interest. This coincided with his estimate of modifications in the bipolar international system. Thus, with reference to NATO, de Gaulle insisted that "America's interests are not always French interests."[9] However, he emphasized that different interests (and, consequently, different policies) need not imply a rejection of the alliance commitment. "Since when in this world," asked Couve de Murville, "have we come to confuse conformism with solidarity."[10] Thus, de Gaulle asserted France's right to remain an American ally on its own terms.

From the inception of the Fifth Republic in 1958 de Gaulle presented to the United States exorbitant demands for greater influence over alliance matters. His memorandum to President Eisenhower in September 1958 proposed that NATO's strategic decisions be made by a directorate composed of France, the United States, and the United Kingdom, and he recommended that NATO's scope be extended beyond Europe. This arrangement would have effected a French veto over the use of nuclear weapons by the United States anywhere in the world. De Gaulle must have known this would be unacceptable to the United States, and he coupled his demands for greater influence in high level alliance planning with accelerated development of France's nuclear deterrent and with limitations on France's participation in NATO.[11] De Gaulle's actions indicated France's resolve to protect its own interests to the extent of dissociating itself from the coordinated operations of the alliance.

Indeed, de Gaulle ultimately defined France's alliance commitment quite narrowly. His argument with the United States over NATO's scope came full circle from his early insistence in his memo to Eisenhower that NATO be extended to non-European areas to his post-1962 attempts to dissociate his country from American policy elsewhere, especially in Vietnam. In de Gaulle's view, Europe was far from ready to enter into an Atlantic partnership in support of America's global policies. On the contrary, he feared involvement in a conflict against his will as a result of France's ties with the United States in NATO. In his words:

While the prospects of a world war breaking out on account of Europe are dissipating, conflicts in which America engages in other parts of the world—as the day before yesterday in Korea, yesterday in Cuba, today in Vietnam—risk, by virtue of that famous escalation, being extended so that the result could be a general conflagration. In that case Europe—whose strategy is, within NATO, that of America—would be automatically involved in the struggle, even when it would not have so desired.[12]

De Gaulle expressed this fear by his progressively stricter definition of France's alliance commitment culminating in the withdrawal of French troops from NATO and the expulsion of NATO headquarters from French territory in 1966. His justifications for this action rested heavily on his interpretation of the altered circumstances since the alliance was formed—the decreased Soviet threat, Europe's recovery, France's independence, and, in particular, the dangers of involvement in non-European wars not of his choosing.[13] On this point, the French memorandum to alliance governments announcing France's withdrawal stated:

It is a fact that Europe is no longer the center of international crises. The center has moved elsewhere, notably in Asia, where all the countries of the Atlantic alliance are obviously not involved.[14]

Thus was the connection between France's withdrawal from NATO and its disapproval of United States policy in Vietnam made explicit.

In addition to terminating French participation in NATO's joint military preparations, de Gaulle presented a narrow interpretation of France's obligations under the alliance: France's duty to assist an ally was to be operative only in cases of "unprovoked aggression."[15] This modification of the North Atlantic Treaty's pledge that "an armed attack against one or more of . . . (the signatories) shall be considered an attack against them all,"[16] emphasized that *France* would determine whether to assist an ally militarily or to support its political positions. To de Gaulle, this French interpretation was the logical extension of national sovereignty which in no way compromised the alliance. To the United States, his posture was a serious limitation of the alliance commitment. The two views are based on different premises: de Gaulle asserted that the French and the American definition of a security threat might not always be in accord; the United States assumed that they would.

As Henry Kissinger has pointed out, de Gaulle's quarrels with the United States were political not technical. They did not concern the arrangements for "sharing" control over nuclear weapons or alliance decision making, but rather the political question of whether the interests of the allies coincided. For example, the Multilateral Force (MLF) proposed by United States President Kennedy after his meeting with British Prime Mininster Macmillan in January 1963 did not meet French demands for more influence in NATO. On the contrary, the proposal for a combined NATO nuclear force was viewed by the French as an American scheme to subjugate the French nuclear deterrent while satiating German ambitions for nuclear weapons. Unable to raise West Germany to the level of France and the United Kingdom, the United States sought to lower the last two to the level of the first.[17] Also, while the MLF entailed surrender of France's entire independent deterrent, the bulk of the American strategic forces would remain independent. French participation was to involve substantially less than British participation; hence, de Gaulle concluded that France was once again to be dominated by Anglo-Saxon hegemony.

Similarly, American prescriptions for burden sharing and particularly the Kennedy administration's emphasis on Atlantic community were viewed with suspicion by de Gaulle since they assumed a harmony of interests between the United States and Europe which, in France's case, did not exist. The United States hinted that equality in NATO would be granted only to a federated Europe and presumed that an "integrated"

Europe would be "outward looking"[18] and would share United States interests. On the contrary, de Gaulle believed that a policy formed on the basis of European national interests would necessarily differ from that of the United States, and he opposed integration as a cloak for subordination. De Gaulle's stubborn opposition to American schemes to unify strategic planning within the alliance or to encourage European federation was interpreted by American officials as the usual Gaullist intransigence. In reality, his objections signified his rejection of continued subordination of French interests to American policy.

By the mid-1960s de Gaulle had concluded that détente had lessened considerably the Soviet threat while American dominance globally rendered the United States as a menace to France. Hence, his opposition to the United States intensified. Withdrawal from NATO's integrated command and the diplomatic nonalignment implied by de Gaulle's restricted definition of the alliance commitment was combined with a strategy of *la défense tous-azimuts,* or defense in all directions. This strategy was introduced in an article by French Chief of Staff Charles Ailleret in the December 1967 issue of *Revue de la Défense Nationale* and endorsed by General de Gaulle in a speech at the Ecole Militaire on January 27, 1968. In brief, it proclaimed that henceforth France's defense

should not be directed in a single direction or at one theoretical enemy, but be able to strike anywhere, that is, it should be all-around, or what we call in military parlance, "all azimuth."[19]

Ailleret's arguments in favor of this strategy focused on two considerations: the impossibility of identifying France's future enemies or allies and the need to provide against intimidation or against France's involvement in a conflict it wished to avoid. Thus the new French strategy was directed against an American menace that was different in kind but not less threatening than the Soviet threat. In its failure to distinguish between ally and enemy, *la défense tous-azimuts* constituted the strategy of a neutral state and therefore represented the corollary of diplomatic nonalignment.[20]

This startling strategic doctrine did not survive the Soviet invasion of Czechoslovakia in August 1968. Reassertion of a Russian menace demanded a recommitment to the principles of NATO and a resurgence of cooperation with the United States.[21] In March 1969, the doctrine of *défense tous-azimuts* was repudiated by an article in *Revue de la Défense Nationale* by General Ailleret's successor, General Fourquet, who not only advocated French-American cooperation against "the enemy from the East,"[22] but also supported the doctrine of flexible response in place of massive retaliation. Since the French forces are capable only of massive reprisals, a doctrine of flexible response relies on other resources in the alliance, particularly those of the United States.

During the last year of de Gaulle's presidency French-American relations enjoyed a tentative renaissance aided by the renewed alliance solidarity that the Soviet invasion of Czechoslovakia demanded, but not limited to it. Also important was the shift in American policy toward the Vietnam conflict which resulted in the Paris peace talks and the advent of the Nixon administration and its new European policy. First, the cessation of the bombing of North Vietnam and a new American peace initiative removed a major source of irritation from French-American relations. Second, President Nixon's avowed intention to respect European interests and independence, and his special efforts to reinvigorate French-American relations during his European tour in March 1969 implied a vindication of de Gaulle's NATO policy.

Under President Georges Pompidou (1969-74), France resumed limited cooperation with NATO forces on an ad hoc basis but did not rejoin NATO. Pompidou's policy seemed more anti-Soviet than that of de Gaulle although he, too, emphasized French independence particularly in monetary matters. Certainly his criticism of the United States was more muted than de Gaulle's. Similarly, Valéry Giscard d'Estaing (1974-present) seems less ambitious globally than de Gaulle and does not emphasize his disagreements with the United States. Nevertheless, his strategic doctrine includes the *force de frappe*, he has not renewed participation in NATO, and he emphasizes France's independent defense policy. Thus, in this crucial area of relations with the United States, French policy during the Fifth Republic has consistently emphasized independence. The harshness of the French critique of American policy varied in tone but not in substance.

The continuing theme of resisting American dominance has characterized French policy since World War II. Its utility to the Fifth Republic should be emphasized: rejection of American hegemony demonstrated the independence of a recovered France. In this sense de Gaulle's policy was united with that of his predecessors and successors. It was, moreover, a policy that was relatively inexpensive and satisfying. As one commentator wrote:

> The ploy (attacking the strongest ally) can be executed at minimum cost and with low risk since a counterattack by the more powerful partner is not likely, considering the larger convergence of interest against the common enemy; if it should occur, the self-fulfilling prophecy can be employed as proof of the major ally's imperial proclivities.[23]

Thus, de Gaulle's critique of United States policy in Vietnam and elsewhere had the positive attribute of illustrating that France was mistress of its own identity with few negative side effects. Indeed, de Gaulle, as he was questioning the American commitment to defend France, relied upon its continuance regardless of his own actions. In his view, the American commitment to defend France would be maintained so long as it was in America's interest and regardless of whether France was a docile ally. The irony of France's situation after World War II was that its ultimate dependence on the United States in defense matters was inescapable.

LEADERSHIP IN EUROPE

De Gaulle's third objective was to pursue leadership in Europe. He hoped to accelerate the trend toward détente and to impede the development of supranationality so as to create the atmosphere most conducive to the exercise of French authority. This required that American and British influence on the continent be restricted, that German power be neutralized, and that France pursue closer relations with the Soviet Union and the other Communist states of Eastern Europe. Thus, de Gaulle's European policy had a dual focus—toward Western Europe's problems in developing as a community and in relating to its American ally and toward the growth of Europe "from the Atlantic to the Urals." The former required continued resistance to American hegemony, and the latter necessitated increased contact between both halves of Europe as well as continued relaxation of tensions between the superpowers.

De Gaulle's hopes to exert French influence on continental European affairs confronted obstacles including the different perceptions of his neighbors regarding key issues, such as European unity or relations with the United States. His opposition to political integration was complete;

he condemned supranational political structures for philosophic and practical reasons. Philosophically, he declared them without foundation in any particular community and, therefore, without legitimacy. Practically, he opposed them because they restricted his freedom of action. Aware of the realities of France's reduced status since World War II, de Gaulle nevertheless sought to reassert French influence without having France absorbed into Europe. For him, French achievements were worthless if they were not uniquely French.

The European theater offered at once the best opportunity for the exercise of French influence and the severest restrictions. France could most legitimately claim a leadership role in a European context; indeed, as one of the original members of the European communities, France's participation was necessary in order to meet the treaty commitments that established them. Hence de Gaulle's tactic of withholding his support from enterprises with which he did not agree was most successful in Europe when he several times boycotted community proceedings in order that France's will prevail. However, the European theater was not without obstacles for the exercise of French influence. France's history had been one of conflict with its neighbors, none of whom was enthusiastic about French dominance of Europe. The same arguments that de Gaulle used so persuasively regarding the United States will to hegemony in Europe could be applied to France by its neighbors.[24]

In the European Economic Community (EEC), de Gaulle found circumstances favorable to the exercise of negative influence whereby a middle power, such as France, withholds its participation from an enterprise not to its liking. French economic interests were most directly affected in the framework of the European Economic Community, and it was imperative to safeguard them, particularly in the difficult negotiations about agricultural policy. Since French participation in the community was vital to the other five members, de Gaulle was able to use forceful methods to France's advantage. The tactics he employed were similar to those he used in NATO—unilateral delineation of French policy, threats to decrease and/or withdraw French participation, etc. In NATO, where French agreement was not as vital as it was in the EEC, this tactic was unsuccessful, and de Gaulle ultimately carried out his threat to withdraw permanently. In the EEC, he was able to force a number of decisions highly favorable to France. He helped move the community toward a common agricultural policy—which benefitted French farmers—and, thus, advanced European economic unity. Political union was another matter. De Gaulle fiercely opposed all attempts to dilute French authority in a supranational organization which, he believed, would be without legitimacy and, inevitably, dependent on the United States. He interpreted American support for European unity and for British entry into the Common Market as further manifestations of American hegemony.

De Gaulle's German policy was the link between his Western and Eastern European policies. European unity was a means of restraining German aggressiveness by encouraging German deference to France in the hope of promoting continental rapprochement. His attitude on the future of Germany was also the basis for his attempt at closer relations with the Soviet Union; he hoped that the traditionally shared desire to contain German ambitions might make cooperation mutually advantageous to France and Russia.[25] Furthermore, he sought to prevent the possibility of *conversations à deux* between the United States and Russia at France's expense.

In a departure from the official Western position, de Gaulle indicated his willingness to accept the Oder-Neisse Line.[26] The traditional Western view had been that acceptance of Germany's frontiers in advance of negotiations would be a unilateral concession to the Soviet Union that would deprive the West Germans of a bargaining point. In contrast, de Gaulle believed that recognition of the Oder-Neisse Line might reassure Germany's neighbors, particularly Poland and the Soviet Union, of its peaceful intentions and remove a potential motive for revanchist military activity. Furthermore, de Gaulle regarded himself as an intermediary between East and West who could reassure the Russians of Germany's peaceful intentions thereby promoting Moscow's interest in an eventual settlement and prompting Bonn to follow Paris's lead.

De Gaulle's Eastern policy met with some success. In June 1966, he became the first Western head of state to visit the Soviet Union since the Russian Revolution; this foreign trip was one of his most important. It celebrated the reopening of a historical friendship without which harmonious continental relations could not exist, and it inaugurated regular consultation between the two countries with a view toward cooperation in a variety of fields.

However, in Europe as elsewhere, de Gaulle's initiatives were subject to substantial limitations. They were influenced by events over which he had little control and they often produced contradictory results. The relation between his policies in Western and Eastern Europe is an interesting case in point. Tensions produced within NATO by French tactics hastened polycentrism in Europe and benefitted de Gaulle's Eastern policy. The Soviet Union was anxious to exploit disintegration in NATO and convinced of Paris's sincerity in seeking to act as an interlocutor with Moscow. However, tensions within NATO, to the extent that they were accompanied by disagreements among the European members of the alliance, tended to defeat de Gaulle's objectives in Western Europe—the construction of an entity independent of the United States.[27] De Gaulle's European alliance partners (especially those in the EEC) whose own policy objectives were in conflict with his regarding immediate and long-term issues (e.g., differences with Germany regarding agricultural policy and reunification, or with Benelux regarding British entry and Atlantic partnership) could only regard his disruptions within NATO with distrust and move closer to the United States. This movement thwarted de Gaulle's goals in Western Europe.

Neither did de Gaulle's Eastern policy always reinforce his objectives. First, de Gaulle had to maintain a certain ambivalence on the subject of Germany lest his rapprochement with the Soviet Union appear to have been completed at the cost of German interests. Germany remained the chief stake in the Soviet-American confrontation in Europe, and the Russians clearly hoped that de Gaulle might support the Soviet position on Germany in its entirety.[28] However, de Gaulle refused to accept the division of Germany as final or to recognize the German Democratic Republic. He could not fully accept the Soviet position without implicitly rejecting the goal of German reunification and alienating the Germans. His vision of continental rapprochement was based on Franco-German friendship and on decreased American influence on the continent. If he had gone too far to embrace his Soviet partner, he would have run the risk of driving the Germans to increased reliance on the United States. Thus, the Franco-Russian dialogue reinforced de Gaulle's policy vis-à-vis the United States and Germany provided it never came to a conclusion, that is, provided the Germans never saw the result of the Franco-Russian dialogue as confirmation of the status quo in Europe.[29]

Second, ambivalence on Germany was necessary from another perspective. French policy toward the East could be seen as the antecedent of Germany's own *Ostpolitik;* de Gaulle could maintain his friendship with Germany by claiming to be Bonn's spokesman in Moscow. However, when

Bonn inaugurated its *Ostpolitik* in the late 1960s, France lost the option of representing Germany to the Soviet Union and Eastern Europe. When asked to comment on Bonn's historic treaty with Poland recognizing the Oder-Neisse Line in 1970, one French official replied: "I'm jealous."[30] The French messenger was no longer necessary.

Third, de Gaulle's policy toward Eastern Europe was at the sufferance of events within the Soviet bloc, since it depended on the existence of strains among Warsaw Pact members which led them to desire increased contacts with the West. Moreover, the limits of such cooperation were set in Moscow and required alleviating the Soviet fear of its consequences.[31] Although some "looseness" within Eastern Europe was necessary in order for positive reception of de Gaulle's overtures to his Eastern neighbors, too much disintegration of the Eastern alliance could promote a Soviet response, such as the Czechoslovakian invasion, and thereby reinforce NATO.

Finally in the area of bipolar détente similar contradictions were apparent. A certain decrease in superpower tension in the era following the Cuban missile crisis enabled de Gaulle to maneuver more freely; on the other hand, too much bipolar rapprochement could result in a duopoly detrimental to French interests. Superpower cooperation was as dangerous to de Gaulle's designs in NATO and Europe as superpower conflict. Thus, the success of de Gaulle's European policies depended on trends and events over which he had little control.

A GLOBAL ROLE

The prime focus of de Gaulle's foreign policy was France's relations with the United States and Europe. However, after 1962, he became concerned with extra-European affairs, in particular, with those involving Third World countries. This shift in emphasis was caused by four factors.

The first was de Gaulle's view of the Cuban missile crisis of 1962 as a turning point in the bipolar confrontation between the United States and the Soviet Union. In his opinion, the post-Cuba era was characterized by increasingly friendly relations between the superpowers and by systemic détente. He concluded that this situation provided ample opportunity for a middle power, such as France, to deemphasize total solidarity with its major ally and to concentrate less on Europe, the focus of Soviet-American conflict.

Second, de Gaulle suspected that in the post-Cuba atmosphere of détente, rapprochement between the United States and the Soviet Union
might lead to a duopoly detrimental to French interests. Tangible evidence
of bipolar cooperation was provided by the Nuclear Test-ban Treaty concluded in August 1963. This agreement, which was inherently discrimin-
atory to emerging nuclear powers, such as France who needed to continue
atmospheric testing, was violently opposed by de Gaulle. His first major
pronouncement regarding American involvement in Vietnam (August 29,
1963) followed the conclusion of the Test-ban Treaty earlier that month.
It can be assumed that the superpower collusion which represented a set-
back to de Gaulle's goal of French-Russian rapprochement was one motive
for de Gaulle's new interest in non-European areas.

Third, by 1963 France had liquidated its colonial dominions in Africa
and settled the Algerian problem and therefore was able to contemplate
a posture of cooperation among Third World states. The protracted Algerian revolt had poisoned French relations with North Africa and the Arab
states throughout its duration. Cast in the role of colonial oppressor,
France could hardly pursue friendly relations with the newly independent
states. The conclusion of the Evian agreements of 1962, which granted
Algeria complete independence and the institution of Franco-Algerian
cooperation based on that principle, permitted France to renew ties with
the Arab countries and to seek to extend French influence elsewhere in
the Third World.

Fourth, by 1963, de Gaulle was faced with a stalemate in the Atlantic
and European areas. Although his policy of rapprochement with Germany
reached a triumphant finale in January 1963 with the conclusion of the
Franco-German Treaty of Friendship and Cooperation, this was the high
point of Franco-German relations; subsequently, their differences often
hampered their cooperation. Furthermore, Western Europe was in disarray
at this time, because of disagreement over supranationality and British
entry into the Common Market, and de Gaulle's bitter rejection of the
MLF revealed the stalemate reached in NATO affairs.

De Gaulle's appeal to less developed or Third World countries assumed
familiar lines: he condemned the exercise of United States hegemony and
urged Third World countries to emulate France's independent policy.
Furthermore, he attempted to maintain a French presence in some less
developed countries and to comment on global issues, such as the 1967
war between the Arabs and Israelis, possibly to involve France in their

resolution. De Gaulle asserted the community of interest between France's preference for a fluid, decentralized international system and the desire of Third World countries for conditions that would permit them to develop economic strength and political independence.[32]

De Gaulle's global policy began with his liquidation of France's control over the vestiges of its empire in Africa and Algeria. During his first four years in office, he granted independence to all the French dependencies in black Africa and to the Algerian rebels. In so doing he attempted to preserve an illusion of continuity that would lay the groundwork for France's future relations with developing countries.

Furthermore, de Gaulle hoped that the example of France's excellent relations with its former colonies would enhance his popularity elsewhere in the Third World. While French military power in Africa is not negligible, de Gaulle relied on an overall policy of economic and political cooperation to perpetuate French influence in the Third World.[33] French economic aid to Algeria and sub-Saharan Africa has been generous; France has consistently led all donor countries including the United States in aid calculated as a percentage of national income. This aid is buttressed by a system of bilateral trade preferences and monetary arrangements with members of the franc zone who also benefit from associated status in the European communities. A major rationale for de Gaulle's post-colonial policy of cooperation was to assure France of the diplomatic support of its former dominions south of the Sahara, whose leaders in the 1960s were men who, schooled in France and conscious of the advantages of cooperating with French policy, were politically conservative and supportive of French policy in international forums.

In addition to his efforts in the former French colonies in Africa, de Gaulle also courted other less developed countries. However, his efforts to promote French influence beyond Africa relied on his personal prestige and his pronouncements rather than on concrete inducements, such as aid. For example, in his 1964 tour of Latin America he exhorted his listeners to follow France's example of independence; his reference to the United States was obvious. However, France's limited resources did not permit de Gaulle to make substantial gains among Third World countries outside of the former French empire.

One important aspect of de Gaulle's Third World policy was his overture to China. This was clearly a response to steps toward Soviet-American cooperation such as the August 1963 Test-ban Treaty. Franco-Chinese

rapprochement heightened French prestige among Third World nations
whose preference for nonalignment caused them to support a challenge
to the Big Two. The United States resented the French move and its timing;[34] hence, de Gaulle was once again demonstrating his independence
from the United States.

The renewal of France's ties with China in January 1964 brought only
limited gains to de Gaulle's policy. France's political influence with the
Peking regime did not significantly rise as a result of recognition. From
1964 to 1969 French-Chinese relations were cool; French representatives
in Peking were subject to the same caprice (including harassment by the
Red Guards and expulsion of journalists) as other diplomatic missions
there. Also, during this period, de Gaulle drew closer to the Soviet Union,
especially after the 1967 Mideast war. China's alleged support for the
French revolutionaries in May-June 1968 did not contribute to cordial
relations between the Chinese and French governments. After 1969 relations between the two countries improved but, clearly, this was determined by China's shifting concept of its interests, rather than as a result
of French moves.

Recognition of China was important in the Vietnam context because
it enabled France to boast of its diplomatic relations with all parties interested in the war. Undoubtedly this was one reason for the selection of
Paris as the site for the Vietnam peace talks. Furthermore, the French
played a role in the renewal of America's contacts with China after 1969.
(This French role is described in Chapter 5.) Prior to 1969, however, the
gains to French policy from de Gaulle's recognition of China were merely
symbolic because of the quixotic nature of Chinese foreign policy.

A final aspect of de Gaulle's global policy was his habit of enunciating
a French position on international issues possibly to promote France's
participation in the resolution of crises, such as the 1967 Mideast war.
However, de Gaulle's preference for advocacy rather than neutrality
destroyed his chances to mediate between the Arabs and Israelis. In 1967
he found fault with Israel for two reasons: first, Israel's initiation of hostilities in disregard of de Gaulle's warning created difficulties for de Gaulle's
attempt to renew French ties with Arab countries after the Algerian settlement. France could no longer balance delicately its Arab and Israeli relations; it was forced to take sides. Second, Israel's initiation of hostilities
and subsequent victory upset the global balance to the disadvantage of
France. The result of the Israeli action was to increase Anglo-American

influence in the Mideast at the expense of the Soviets whose Arab clients were so swiftly defeated. In de Gaulle's view, this increased the gap between the superpowers to the further advantage of the United States. Thus de Gaulle's concern extended beyond the immediate area and involved his fear of increasing American neo-imperialism. In addition, the Mideast tension might have produced either a clash between the superpowers involving their respective allies, or a solution imposed by the Big Two that might prejudice French interests. Israeli action thus evoked de Gaulle's two nightmares, superpower collision or collusion.[35]

De Gaulle's policy following the 1967 war was clearly anti-Israeli. On June 5, 1967, when hostilities broke out, de Gaulle announced suspension of arms shipments to both sides. Had this embargo been applied evenly, it would nevertheless have penalized Israel, which alone received most of its arms from France. In fact, it was gradually redefined to permit arms shipments to several Arab countries, while Israel, after its January 1969 raid on the Beirut airport, was almost completely cut off.

De Gaulle's leniency toward the Arabs may be partially explained by the increase in France's arms sales to Arab countries and by the necessity to secure favorable access to oil. Arms trade has traditionally been a source of political influence; thus, through increased sales to Arab states, de Gaulle attempted to create future political leverage. Also, the French arms industry, whose death would spell doom for France's independent defense, needs to export in order to survive. Therefore, courting Arab markets is simply good business.

In the case of oil, France sought to diversify its oil suppliers so as to increase its independence vis-à-vis the Anglo-American oil trusts and to assure a continued supply regardless of whether the Suez Canal were open or relations with Algeria continued to be friendly. This coincided with de Gaulle's wider aim of increasing France's independence and replacing American influence with his own; de Gaulle knew that in November 1956 the United States had threatened to cut off the oil flowing to France and Britain unless they withdrew their forces from Suez.[36]

Since de Gaulle's policy after the 1967 war clearly favored the Arabs, there were no prospects for a French mediatory role in the Mideast. Prior to the 1967 war, de Gaulle had been the only Western statesman who inspired some confidence among both Arabs and Israelis, due to his attempts to rebuild France's ties with Arab states after the 1962 Algerian settlement. However, he forfeited this position in the months after the war so that, unwelcome in Washington and Tel Aviv, he became less valuable in Cairo.[37]

De Gaulle's Mideast policy, in which he chose advocacy rather than neutrality, bears witness to the narrow field within which he could operate when confronted with conflicting small power aims in the shadow of superpower involvement. The Arab-Israeli situation seemed well suited to the exercise of a constructive French role as potential mediator and guarantor. Nevertheless, French participation in a settlement in whatever capacity depended upon a convergence of national wills as well as skillful manipulation of circumstances. In this case, there was neither.

VIETNAM AND DE GAULLE'S FOREIGN POLICY

France's critique of American policy in Vietnam from 1963 to 1973 reflected de Gaulle's perceptions of international affairs as well as his three main foreign policy objectives. Primarily, de Gaulle viewed Vietnam as an opportunity to demonstrate France's independence from the United States. American policy in Vietnam represented the kind of situation from which de Gaulle hoped to exclude France; he disapproved of the war and feared that it would widen, involving France and other NATO members against their will. Such restrictions on France's decision-making capacity in defense situations were intolerable to de Gaulle and were his stated reasons for withdrawing from NATO.

The impression that an alliance of states located mainly in the Atlantic area would involve its members in Asian conflicts did not originate with de Gaulle. In the decade after the North Atlantic Treaty was signed in 1949, NATO became the cornerstone of the global American strategy to contain Communism after World War II. Its members viewed the Atlantic Alliance as an affirmation of their solidarity in non-European areas. Thus, the United States during the Korean struggle and France during the 1946-54 Indochina war claimed that the common enemy was being fought. This extension of NATO's scope beyond Europe was not without benefit to the European states in the 1950s: West Germany regained sovereignty and the right to rearm as a result of the Korean War, and France received United States financial support in its struggle in Indochina. However, in the 1960s, the European states' global interests receded with the loss of their colonies, while United States influence expanded. In view of the disparity between their own narrowing interests and broadening United

States concerns, the Europeans, especially de Gaulle, were reluctant in the 1960s to regard NATO as the core of a united global front against Communism.

Second, de Gaulle's Vietnam policy was prompted by the same visions of an evolving bipolar system that inspired his European policy. He viewed the Vietnam war in the context of muted bipolarity and, therefore, rejected containment of monolithic Communism as a rationale for the American presence in Southeast Asia. His own recognition of the People's Republic of China signified de Gaulle's belief in the end of bipolarity in Asia; he argued that the United States should, likewise, cease operating under narrow ideological constraints.

Moreover, de Gaulle chose to regard Vietnam's quest for independence as similar to France's pursuit of the same goal. He meant independence from great power influence rather than from the socialist/capitalism dichotomy and therefore his analysis differed sharply from that of the United States which assumed the persistence of cold war animosities.

In Europe, de Gaulle viewed ideology as transient and subordinate to national interest; hence, he sought to increase France's ties with the Soviet Union and with its Warsaw Pact allies. In Asia, de Gaulle's view of the prominence of national interest led to his scepticism regarding United States policy. He saw no possible gains for the United States in pursuit of a policy that opposed national interest. On the contrary, American policy in Asia carried a triple threat: it might instigate conflict involving France; it might escalate to a major war involving China and other Asian powers; or, it might perpetuate an American colony in Asia. In any of these cases, de Gaulle found American policy in Vietnam objectionable.

Third, France's Vietnam policy parallelled de Gaulle's quest for a global role. Not only did Gaullist pronouncements on Vietnam represent France's independent foreign policy, they also promoted the image of France's global concerns and the desirability of French participation in eventual peace talks. Thus, de Gaulle's policy in Vietnam was part of his post-1963 attempt to reassert France's traditional global interests. A former French colony, Vietnam became in the 1960s the victim of de Gaulle's constant obsession: American hegemony. It was natural that he extend France's plea for global influence to the Vietnam situation.

De Gaulle's own experiences with the forces of national liberation in Algeria supported his conviction that decolonization was inevitable. He realized that the United States was opposing nationalism in Vietnam and that victory was not possible. Undoubtedly he hoped that his Vietnam stance would increase France's prestige in the Third World.

Finally, de Gaulle's Vietnam policy reflected his foreign policy style. He preferred dramatic declarative statements that were calculated to be shocking in timing, tone, and content. Such pronouncements were in themselves illustrations of France's independent foreign policy positions and were intended as such. As Stanley Hoffmann has written:

The style was the policy; the style could hardly be imagined on behalf of a less ambitious policy, and it would have been difficult to wage his policy in a self-effacing style. . . . Yet the policy was more than the style.[38]

De Gaulle's preference for dramatic public statements was at odds with the quiet persuasion that might have convinced the United States of its errors in Vietnam (although the British were not successful with such a quiet approach). However, such private maneuvers were not suited to de Gaulle's personal political style and to his larger goal of demonstrating France's independence from the United States.

De Gaulle's anti-American rhetoric reached a crescendo during the American involvement in Vietnam. Now that the Indochinese war is over, his harsh critique of American policy can be put in perspective. A dispassionate examination of French policy toward Vietnam from 1963 to 1973 indicates its relation to the central themes of the Gaullist approach to foreign affairs. Moreover, disagreements between France and the United States in Southeast Asia during the 1960s and 1970s echoed their historic discord there. This earlier period in Indochinese history will now be examined.

NOTES

1. Indispensable to an understanding of de Gaulle's philosophy and foreign policy are Stanley Hoffmann's writings, particularly, *Decline or Renewal? France Since the 1930s* (New York: Viking Press, 1974), Parts III and IV.

2. The Cuban missile crisis has been cited as the beginning of the period of détente by several scholars. For examples, see Dan Caldwell, "Détente in Historical Perspective," *International Studies Notes*, 3, 4 (Winter 1976), p. 19.

3. Alfred Grosser, *French Foreign Policy Under de Gaulle* (Boston: Little, Brown, & Co., 1967), pp. 37-46, and Dorothy Pickles, *Algeria and France: From Colonialism to Cooperation* (New York: Praeger, 1963).

4. This reasoning was made explicit by Jean de Broglie, Secretary of State for Algerian Affairs in a speech on November 4, 1964, when he said:

> Algeria is also and certainly the *"porte étroite"* by which we penetrate the Third World. A quarrel between France and another state in North Africa is only a simple bilateral tension. A quarrel with Algeria exceeds the limits of Franco-Algerian relations and threatens to destroy the efforts of our diplomacy in the entire world.

Quoted in Guy de Carmoy, *Les Politiques Etrangères de La France 1944-1966* (Paris: La Table Ronde, 1967), p. 292.

5. For a discussion of the elements of continuity and change in foreign policy goals under the Fourth and Fifth Republics, see Jean-Baptiste Duroselle, "Changes in French Foreign Policy since 1945," in Stanley Hoffmann, ed., *In Search of France* (Cambridge: Harvard University Press, 1963); also Raymond Aron, *France Steadfast and Changing: The Fourth to the Fifth Republic* (Cambridge, Mass.: Harvard University Press, 1960); and Grosser, *French Foreign Policy.*

6. Lawrence Scheinman, *Atomic Energy in France Under the Fourth Republic* (Princeton: Princeton University Press, 1965), p. 217. Scheinman's book is the classic study of the *force de frappe*'s origins.

7. Philip Williams, *Crisis and Compromise: Politics in the Fourth Republic* (Garden City: Doubleday, 1966).

8. Raymond Aron, "From Independence to Neutrality," *Atlantic Community Quarterly,* 6, no. 1 (Spring 1968), pp. 267-269. (Reprinted from *Revue de la Défense Nationale,* December 1967.)

9. Remarks by General de Gaulle at weekly meeting of Council of Ministers, January 7, 1963, quoted in André Passeron, *De Gaulle Parle: 1962-1966* (Paris: Fayard, 1966), p. 201.

10. Former French Foreign Minister Maurice Couve de Murville, addressing the French National Assembly, October 29, 1963, reprinted in *Vital Speeches,* 30, no. 3 (November 15, 1963), p. 75.

11. De Gaulle spoke of France's goal of an independent deterrent in a speech at the Ecole Militaire in November 1959. In March of that year, he had announced that the French Mediterranean Fleet would be withdrawn from the NATO command in wartime and that certain areas (e.g., the Middle East, North Africa, black Africa) were not included in the NATO system, implying that France would follow an independent policy there. In July 1959, de Gaulle refused French participation in an integrated alert and air defense system. Thus, his early demands for more influence within the alliance were combined with measures decreasing French participation in its activities.

12. Thirteenth Press Conference, February 21, 1966, *Major Addresses, Statements and Press Conferences of General Charles de Gaulle: March 17, 1964-May 16, 1967* (New York: French Embassy, 1967), vol. 2, p. 118.

13. See Texts of French Memoranda to NATO Allies, March 8, 10, 29, and 30, 1966, *French Affairs No. 192* (New York: French Embassy, 1966). Also, see de Gaulle's press conference of February 21, 1966, and Pompidou's statements before the French National Assembly on April 13 and 14, 1966.

14. Text of French Memorandum of March 8 and 10, 1966, p. 2.

15. Premier Georges Pompidou addresses the French National Assembly,

April 20, 1966. *Speeches and Press Conferences,* No. 245 (New York, French Embassy, 1966), p. 12.

16. North Atlantic Treaty, April 4, 1949, Article 5, reprinted in Edwin H. Fedder, *NATO: The Dynamics of Alliance in Postwar World* (New York: Dodd, Mead and Co., 1973), Appendix.

17. Jacques Vernant, "La Crise du Vietnam et la Dilemme Nucléaire," *Revue de la Défense Nationale,* 22 (January 1966), p. 135. Raymond Aron has pointed out that, since the Nassau proposal "implicitly put France on the same footing as Great Britain," it could have been regarded as victory for de Gaulle's diplomacy, *The Great Debate: Theories of Nuclear Strategy* (New York: Anchor Books, 1965), p. 95. Simon Serfaty, *France, De Gaulle, and Europe* (Baltimore: Johns Hopkins University Press, 1968), p. 126, makes this same point.

18. Henry Kissinger, *The Troubled Partnership: A Re-appraisal of the Atlantic Alliance* (New York: McGraw-Hill, 1965), p. 36.

19. Charles Louis Ailleret, "Defense in All Directions," *Atlantic Community Quarterly,* 4, no. 1 (Spring 1968), p. 24. (Reprinted from *Revue de la Défense Nationale,* December 1967.)

20. Aron, "From Independence to Neutrality," p. 267.

21. Guy de Carmoy wrote that "according to certain sources, Franco-American conversations on possible future collaboration in the field of nuclear weapons are said to have been started at the end of 1968," in "The Last Year of de Gaulle's Foreign Policy," *International Affairs* (July 1969) p. 426. A similar report that ascribed the desire to cooperate with the United States on nuclear weapons to certain French army officers was quoted from *Le Monde* in the *Washington Post,* January 5, 1969, p. A12. De Gaulle may have acceded to the wishes of these officers whose support he had required during the civil disturbances of May and June 1968.

22. de Carmoy, "The Last Year of de Gaulle's Foreign Policy," p. 426.

23. Edward A. Kolodziej, *France's International Policy from de Gaulle to Pompidou,* (Ithaca, N.Y.: Cornell University Press, 1974), p. 52.

24. Edward A. Kolodziej, "France and the Atlantic Alliance: Alliance with a De-Aligning Power," *Polity,* 2, no. 3 (Spring 1970), pp. 249-254. For a discussion of some of these European differences, see Stanley Hoffmann, *Gulliver's Troubles* (New York: McGraw-Hill, 1968), pp. 406-458.

25. De Gaulle's attempts to promote Franco-Russian cooperation began during World War II when he journeyed to Moscow in 1944. "Perhaps it would be possible," he wrote of his hopes for the trip, "to renew the old Franco-Russian solidarity which, though repeatedly betrayed and repudiated, remained no less a part of the natural order of things, as much in relation to the German menace as to the endeavors of Anglo-American hegemony," *The War Memoirs of Charles de Gaulle,* vol. 3, *Salvation 1944-1946* (New York: Simon and Schuster, 1960), p. 61. Reportedly, after meeting with Stalin, de Gaulle referred to him as "the Tsar." He liked to use the term "Russia" instead of "the Soviet Union" with the intention of emphasizing the persistence of a historic national entity with its own identity, interests, and ambitions irrespective of modern ideologies. While cold war animosity persisted, de Gaulle proclaimed French friendship for Russians noting the absence of "feeling of competition or animosity toward the Russian people." March 25, 1959. *Major Addresses, Statements and Press Conferences of General Charles de Gaulle:*

May 19, 1958-January 31, 1964 (New York: French Embassy, 1964), vol. 1, p. 44.

26. Eleventh Press Conference, February 4, 1965, *Major Addresses,* vol. 2, p. 85. Previously, in his press conference of March 25, 1959, de Gaulle had seemed to favor acceptance of the Oder-Neisse line, *Major Addresses,* vol. 1, p. 43.

Simon Serfaty notes that since French interests were well served by the status quo in Germany, de Gaulle could at the same time be tough regarding Berlin, refuse to recognize the German Democratic Republic, and admit the permanence of present frontiers. *France, De Gaulle, and Europe,* p. 131.

27. In André Fontaine's analysis, de Gaulle is to be praised for "going beyond containment" and faulted for "believing this can be done without the concerted cooperation of all the allies." *Le Monde,* February 11, 1965, pp. 1, 3.

28. André Fontaine discusses Russian intentions regarding de Gaulle in "L 'Europe et l'Asie," *Le Monde,* March 9, 1965, p. 1.

29. Raymond Aron, "Tour de Valse," *Le Figaro,* April 1, 1965, pp. 1, 32.

30. Quoted by Charles R. Tanguy, interviewed in Washington, D.C., January 15, 1971. Mr. Tanguy, an American Foreign Service Officer, was attached to the American embassy in Paris from 1964 to 1968 and was country director for France and Benelux at the Department of State from 1968 to 1972.

31. *Le Monde* expressed doubts about France's Eastern policy "which, in contrast to that which she practices in the West, seeks simultaneously the destruction of hegemony and the development of good relations with the hegemonic powers." Editorial, November 4, 1965, p. 1, after Couve de Murville's trip to Russia.

32. He cautioned lest the less developed countries become "areas of competition and possible battlefields for the great imperialist nations of today and tomorrow." Ninth Press Conference, January 31, 1964, *Major Addresses,* vol. 1, p. 252.

33. The agreements concluded between France and its former colonies in Africa provide that France may intervene militarily if this is requested by the existing African governments. For a statement of French policy by a French civil servant, see M. Daniel Pepy, "France's Relations with Africa," *African Affairs,* 59, no. 275 (April 1970), pp. 155-162. Also on this subject, see Keith Irvine, "Franczone Africa," *Current History,* 56, no. 333 (May 1969), pp. 282-285.

34. Reportedly, American Ambassador to France Charles Bohlen had urged de Gaulle to postpone recognition until after the American elections in November 1964 and had received some assurance along these lines. Hence, the two-month-old Johnson administration was displeased when recognition was extended in January 1964 and suspected that the move was intended to embarrass the United States.

35. Stanley Hoffmann, "Minimum Feasible Misunderstanding: America and France," *New Republic,* 160 (April 5, 1969), p. 20.

36. Robert Gilpin, *U.S. Power and the Multinational Corporation,* (New York: Basic Books, 1975), p. 149. Gilpin notes that "this experience is one the French have not forgotten."

37. Raymond Aron, *De Gaulle, Israel, et Les Juifs* (Paris: Plon, 1968), p. 26.

38. Hoffmann, *Decline or Renewal?,* p. 287.

Part II | HISTORICAL FACTORS

Chapter 2

The Roots of French-American Discord over Vietnam

France's reaction to American involvement in Vietnam in the 1960s was rooted in an earlier historical period. Undoubtedly, the erosion of their rule in Indochina[1] during World War II and their subsequent defeat by the Viet Minh impressed the French with the futility of opposing Vietnamese nationalism. Furthermore, American ambivalence regarding France's efforts to reassert its authority in Indochina in 1945-46 aroused resentment among French leaders. In particular, General de Gaulle, who headed the French Provisional Government in 1945, was frustrated and angered by American policy in this regard. Unfortunately, French-American differences deepened as the Indochina war progressed. Finally, at the 1954 Geneva conference, the French were dismayed by what they regarded as a lack of American diplomatic support. All of these experiences contributed to French skepticism about subsequent American policy in Vietnam.

THE OUTBREAK OF WAR IN INDOCHINA

FRENCH RULE IN INDOCHINA IS INTERRUPTED

It is instructive to recall the events leading up to the first Indochina war before examining how French and American policy there differed from 1940 to 1954. During World War II, the exercise of French sovereignty over Indochina was interrupted for the first time in nearly seventy years. In 1940, the representatives of Vichy France in Indochina and the Japanese concluded a series of collaboration agreements that allowed French forces to remain nominally in control. However, on March 9, 1945, as the war in the Pacific neared its end, the Japanese moved suddenly to disarm the French. Two days later, they set up a puppet regime under Vietnamese Emperor Bao Dai who declared Vietnam independent of France.

Hence, the immediate goal of the French in 1945 was to reassert their authority in Indochina as quickly as possible. Toward that end, on March 24, 1945, General de Gaulle announced the creation of the Indochinese Federation, which was to have a new status within the French community.[2] However, events continued to overtake French policy. Before the French could regain power from the Japanese, an indigenous group, led by Ho Chi Minh and strengthened by the confusing situation of the war years, had come to power in the northern area of Vietnam.

Ho had spent the years between 1938 and 1945 in China; he returned to Vietnam in May 1945.[3] He and his guerrillas increased their activity against the Japanese and set up "peoples' regimes" in six Vietnamese provinces. On September 2, 1945, they proclaimed the birth of the Democratic Republic of Vietnam. Bao Dai renounced his imperial title and became a counselor to the new government. The existence of this rival regime in Tonkin complicated the task of the returning French. Aware of the difficulties of the situation, General de Gaulle ordered General Leclerc, his appointed commander of the French forces in Asia, to proceed first to Cochinchina, postponing occupation of Tonkin until later. Before the war, Cochinchina, the southernmost part of Vietnam, had been administered directly by the French because of their important economic interests there; it was also the area in which Ho Chi Minh and his followers, who became known as the Viet Minh, were weakest. In contrast, the northernmost sector, Tonkin, was the site of the Viet Minh headquarters in Hanoi and the area of its greatest strength. De Gaulle correctly assumed that the returning French forces would meet far less opposition in the south than in the north.

Tonkin was not reoccupied by the French until March 1946, two months after de Gaulle had retired temporarily from French politics. However, he had laid down to General Leclerc three conditions to be fulfilled before the French returned to the north. These were: "(that) the situation be clarified, the population thoroughly exasperated by the presence of the Chinese, and relations settled between (de Gaulle's representative) Sainteny and Ho Chi Minh."[4]

By March 1946, all three of de Gaulle's conditions were fulfilled.[5] First, the Vietnamese government seemed to have control over the major parts of Tonkin and Annam. Moreover, French representatives in the area, including Pierre Messmer, then a French official who parachuted into Vietnam in August 1945 (and later premier of France under Georges Pompidou), and Jean Sainteny, the French commissioner for Tonkin and Annam (1945-47), attested to the fact that Ho Chi Minh and his collaborators had captured considerable public support.

Second, the Vietnamese were fed up with the Chinese occupation. Chinese troops had arrived in the northern sector of Vietnam in September 1945 in accord with the Allied agreement at Potsdam the previous July. Simultaneously, British troops had occupied the southern sector of Vietnam for the Allies.

The Chinese occupation was officially neutral between the Vietnamese revolutionaries and the French; hence, the Chinese incurred the wrath of both parties. The French did not believe that the Chinese were energetic enough in hastening the restoration of French sovereignty.[6] They preferred the actions of the British who, led by General Gracey, assisted General Leclerc in the reassertion of French authority in the south and promptly withdrew in December 1945. In contrast, the Chinese did not evacuate their troops from the north until June 1946. By this time, the Vietnamese were equally disillusioned with the Chinese occupation force. The Chinese government had refused to recognize Ho Chi Minh's government, so that its neutral policy actually acknowledged the ultimate return of the French.

The Vietnamese leaders, who had spent most of the war years in China, had hoped for a more sympathetic attitude on the part of the Chinese.[7] This failing, the Vietnamese were happy to see the Chinese leave. As Ho Chi Minh told Paul Mus: "It is better to smell the feces of the French for a little while than to eat Chinese excrement all of one's life."[8]

Third, by March 1946, the rapport between the French representative in Hanoi, Jean Sainteny, and Ho Chi Minh made an accord possible. Sainteny, a French businessman in Indochina before the war and later a member of the resistance, was assigned in 1945 by General de Gaulle to lead a French mission in Kun-ming, China; his goal was to return French authority to Indochina as quickly as possible. Sainteny and a few comrades arrived in Hanoi at the moment when Ho Chi Minh was setting up his government in August and September 1945. Sainteny became well acquainted with Ho, and the two men held a series of private nocturnal meetings to negotiate the French return to northern Vietnam. Sainteny and Ho reached an accord, which they signed on behalf of their governments on March 6, 1946. Its first provision read:

The French government recognizes the republic of Vietnam as a free state having its government, its parliament, its army and its finances, forming part of the Indochinese Federation and the French Union. In that which concerns the Union of the three "Kys," the French government agrees to ratify the decisions taken by the populations consulted by referendum.[9]

The French had made two important concessions. First, they acknowledged that Vietnam was entitled to the status of a "free state," implying an independent character. Second, they promised not to interfere with the unity of the three kys of Vietnam (Tonkin, Annam, and Cochinchina) which would be decided by referendum. In return, the Vietnamese agreed to postpone the exercise of independence and "to welcome amicably the (returning) French army."[10]

The vague terms of the March 6 accord were to be interpreted into specific arrangements during future meetings between the two sides. However, these negotiations were beset with difficulties; at meetings in Dalat, Vietnam, and Fontainebleu, France, in the summer of 1946, it became clear that the French and Vietnamese were not prepared to negotiate on the same basis.

The Vietnamese regarded the provisions of the March 6 accord as the principles on which future agreements would be based; they saw the accord as a beginning. They agreed to less than complete independence because they relied on French promises to proceed toward that goal. French recalcitrance at subsequent meetings caused the Vietnamese to feel betrayed. Further evidence of France's bad faith was its cooperation in the establishment of an independent republic in Cochinchina on June 1, 1946, as the Fontainebleu conference opened. This action directly violated the French promise on March 6 to preserve the unity of the three kys.

Clearly, the French viewed the March 6 accord as the maximum they would agree to in order that their returning troops meet no armed resistance from the Vietnamese. The French army occupied the northern area of Vietnam on March 18, 1946; once reinstated on Vietnamese territory, they were inclined to take the narrowest interpretation of their concessions to Vietnamese independence. They viewed the Vietnamese position at the Dalat and Fontainebleu conferences as an attempt to obtain further concessions beyond the terms of the prior accord. Therefore, agreement between the two sides was impossible.

Ho Chi Minh, who had traveled to France for the Fontainebleu meetings, was disappointed at the failure to reach a satisfactory accord. In September 1946, he beseeched his friend Sainteny not to let him return to his country empty-handed. Nevertheless, the modus vivendi signed by Ho and French Overseas Minister Marius Moutet on September 14 was no substitute for a detailed and binding agreement.

In the months following Ho Chi Minh's return to Vietnam, the situation rapidly deteriorated. Fighting broke out in November in Haiphong, a major port where Vietnamese and French forces coexisted uneasily. After several incidents involving conflicts over exercise of the customs function, the military commander in Haiphong, Colonel Dèbes, issued an impossible ultimatum to the Vietnamese forces, leaving them only two hours to comply. When they failed to do so, he opened fire using land and naval artillery. In response, General Vo Nguyen Giap led the Vietnamese in a large-scale surprise attack against the French in Hanoi on December 19, 1946. The first Indochina war had begun.[11]

THE LOST PEACE

Sainteny's account of the events of 1945-46 is titled "History of a Lost Peace" (*paix manquée*); this phrase suggests that the outbreak of hostilities might have been avoided. However, the events of the period from March 1945, when the Japanese disarmed the French, to December 1946, when full-scale war erupted between the French and the Vietnamese, moved with the rhythm of a Greek tragedy. Armed conflict seemed inevitable even though moderates, such as Ho Chi Minh and Jean Sainteny, hoped for a peaceful solution incorporating both Vietnamese and French interests. In spite of efforts to reach such a solution, the extremists on both sides prevailed; they had several compelling advantages.

First, the moderates were a very small group. It is probably an exaggeration to argue that many of France's leaders were prepared to give

Vietnam complete independence, even in a distant future. Even those Frenchmen with some sympathy for the Vietnamese cause envisioned a continuing dependence on France. In turn, the extreme elements in Vietnam were strengthened by French recalcitrance on the independence issue.

Second, the French commanders in the field were ardent colonialists who were eager to reassert forceably French authority in Vietnam. Colonel Dèbes, who ordered the French attack at Haiphong on November 23, disliked the Vietnamese and they "thoroughly detested" him.[12] With such lack of sympathy for the Vietnamese on the part of local French officials, it is doubtful that violence could have been avoided.

Third, the instability of the French government prevented the adoption of a consistent policy toward Vietnam after World War II, especially one that recognized the Vietnamese desire for self-determination. Four men headed the French government in 1946; Charles de Gaulle, who resigned in January; Félix Gouin, who held power from January to June; Georges Bidault, who was in office from June to December; and Léon Blum, who succeeded Bidault. De Gaulle and Bidault were pro-colonialist, while Gouin and Blum were inclined to favor national self-determination. Governmental instability, which became typical of the Fourth Republic, caused these four men of different persuasions to alternate in office during 1946: first a colonialist, then an anti-colonialist, and so on. The Gouin government approved of the March 6 accord with the Vietnamese; the Bidault government did not and hence did nothing to facilitate agreement with the Vietnamese at Fontainebleu in July.[13] When Blum took over in December, it was too late to avert violence. The unstable political situation in Paris had strengthened the extremists on both sides and hastened the outbreak of war.

Furthermore, continued governmental instability gave the war its hopeless character. The goal of retaining Vietnam as a French colony was unrealistic in view of Ho Chi Minh's military and political strength. After 1949, France supported a rival regime led by Bao Dai but refused to grant him the independence that would have been the condition of his success.[14] Yet the French were unable to shift to a more realistic policy. This lack of direction and coherence was endemic to a political system in which successive coalition governments postponed decisions rather than risk loss of parliamentary support. The natural advocates of Vietnamese independence, Communists and Socialists, had been handicapped by the necessity of maintaining their positions in the French government. Communist participation in cabinets prior to 1947 silenced the extreme Left at the moment when, in the spring and summer of 1946, Ho Chi Minh tried to negotiate a solution. Later governments remained divided on this issue and resisted major changes of direction in the Indochina policy as elsewhere. Thus, "the war was not directed at all. Because the government was divided and its plans were confused, the war was fought without a goal."[15]

SEPARATE FRENCH-AMERICAN PERSPECTIVES IN SOUTHEAST ASIA, 1940-54

WARTIME PLANNING AND ALLIED OCCUPATION OF VIETNAM

The first juncture at which French and American policy over Vietnam conflicted was during wartime planning. President Franklin D. Roosevelt was convinced that France's inability to defend Indochina destroyed its right to regain control of its colony.

When France fell to the Germans in June 1940, the United States was officially neutral in the war between Allied and Axis powers; its policy in the Far East was governed by this fact and by the belief that the Japanese would not use force against the French in Indochina. These latter calculations were disproved when in September 1940 the Japanese attacked two French fortresses inflicting 800 casualties on the brave but hopelessly outnumbered French garrisons. Although the Vichy regime had no alternative but to conclude an agreement permitting the Japanese to station troops in Indochina, in the minds of Allied statesmen French collaboration was regarded somewhat resentfully.[16]

President Roosevelt's view that Indochina should be placed under international trusteeship was well-known. In January 1944, he bluntly remarked to the British ambassador to the United States, Lord Halifax: "for over a year, (I have) expressed the opinion that Indochina should not go back to France but that it should be administered by an international trusteeship."[17] Furthermore, Roosevelt had discussed the future of Indochina with the Chinese at Cairo and with the Russians at Teheran, that is, in forums where no representative of France was present. Finally, this American attitude was in sharp contrast to frequent American promises that France would retain control of its colonies after the war.[18]

Naturally, General de Gaulle, head of the French Provisional Government, was furious over this American attitude. In addition, he was frustrated by Washington's refusal to provide transport to the Far East for the French troops training in Africa and Madagascar despite, in his words, "the incessant representations of the French government."[19] The French later blamed this United States refusal for the delay in their return to Indochina.

Meeting in Potsdam in July 1945, the Allies (without France) decided that Indochina should be divided for the purpose of occupation at the sixteenth parallel; occupation duties north of this line fell to the Chinese and south of it to the British. The decision to divide the country at that point was due to military considerations; the nature and location of the boundary between the two halves of Vietnam would later become a controversial political question.

General de Gaulle objected to the Potsdam arrangement on the grounds that French troops should be the agents of liberation in the French colonies and because he believed that China's reluctance to permit the complete restoration of French control in Indochina might lead the Chinese authorities to sympathize with indigenous revolutionary movements.[20]

Events seemed to confirm de Gaulle's apprehensions in the latter regard. It was in the Chinese sector that Ho Chi Minh proclaimed an independent Vietnamese republic. The officially neutral Chinese, whose policy left Ho dissatisfied, nevertheless permitted the rebel government to exist. Furthermore, as mentioned previously, Chinese officials in Hanoi, led by General Lu Han who did not agree with his government's neutral policy, made life difficult for the French mission in Hanoi under Jean Sainteny.

United States officials, especially Colonel Patti, head of the Office of Strategic Services (OSS) in south China, had frustrated French efforts to reassert control in Indochina since the Japanese moved against the French in March 1945. At that time, the retreating French forces in Indochina asked Sainteny (then head of the French mission at Kun-ming, China) for air cover. He relayed the request to Major General Claire L. Chennault, Commander, Fourteenth United States Air Force who refused on orders from Washington.[21] Furthermore, Colonel Patti repeatedly delayed Sainteny's return to Indochina; in Sainteny's words: "he did all he could to stop me."[22]

When he finally reached Hanoi in August 1945 Sainteny found himself a virtual prisoner, though, as he put it, in a gilded cage.[23] His movements watched, unable to make contact with the French population of Hanoi, and forbidden to fly the French flag, Sainteny found it difficult to attain his objective, viz., the reassertion of French authority in Vietnam. In the eyes of the Allies, "the representatives of France at Hanoi, on French territory, (were) . . . only a simple mission, openly ignored, systematically obstructed by a constant sly hostility."[24] Thus, Allied policy, for which the United States was particularly responsible, undermined French authority in its own colony.

Furthermore, the French believed that the United States supported the Vietnamese revolutionaries. The OSS had contacted Ho Chi Minh while the latter was in China, and, during the period from July to September 1945, the OSS supplied Ho with a small quantity of small arms.[25] At the national day celebration in Hanoi on September 2, 1946, two American planes flew overhead during the ceremony, a signal to the Vietnamese gathered below of American sympathy for their cause. All of these signs convinced the French that the United States had adopted an anti-colonialist position in Vietnam in disregard of France's interests.[26]

UNITED STATES SUPPORT FOR FRANCE DURING THE FIRST INDO-
CHINA WAR

American policy gradually became more sympathetic to the French position in Indochina. An important factor in this connection was the British attitude. Itself a colonial power, Britain defended France's right to participate in the liberation of Indochina and, during the wartime conferences, refused to agree to an Allied declaration on colonial self-government. Under British influence, the United States decided, early in 1945, that Indochina's fate should be left in France's hands.[27]

The shift in American policy from insistence on the concept of international trusteeship to a willingness to let France determine the fate of its Indochina colony was indicated by President Roosevelt's statement of April 3, 1945. Referring to the Yalta Conference, Roosevelt stated that the United States felt trusteeship should be the status of the territories mandated after World War I, those taken from the enemy in World War II, and "such other territories as might *voluntarily* be placed under trusteeship."[28] In the French view, especially that of General de Gaulle who headed the French government at that time, this belated American willingness to defer to France on a matter concerning a French colony was far from reassuring.

After the outbreak of hostilities, the United States urged the French to deal positively with the nationalist aspirations of the Vietnamese in order to avoid a protracted conflict. Nonetheless, American policy continued to defer to the French regarding Indochina. The final shift in American policy—from deference to France to active support of the French war effort—took place in early 1950. At that time, France granted the Bao Dai government a degree of autonomy and requested United States aid. The French argued that active support for their forces was the only way to oppose the spread of Asian Communism in Indochina.

The United States commitment to aid the victims of Soviet Communist aggression had been spelled out in sweeping terms by President Truman in March 1947; however, the Truman Doctrine was not immediately applied to Asia. In fact, United States intelligence estimates could find no evidence linking Ho Chi Minh to Soviet Communism. As late as the fall of 1948, a report of the Intelligence and Research Division of the United States State Department could find no direct links between Vietnamese and Russian Communists and could offer no explanation for their absence.[29]

The Communist victory in China in December 1949 provided the necessary "proof" that the Soviets were spreading their system of government to Asia. Henceforth, direct ties or not, it became necessary to defeat Ho Chi Minh. Two months after Mao's victory, the United States recognized the Bao Dai regime and, in May 1950, stated its willingness to support substantially the French/Bao Dai forces. On May 11, 1950, Secretary of State Acheson announced plans to implement a $60 million program of economic and technical assistance to Southeast Asia together with an undisclosed amount of military aid. Thus, a month before the start of the Korean War, the United States was committed to oppose Communism in Asia.

From 1950, when its support of the French effort solidified, until 1954 when France signed an armistice with the Viet Minh, the United States pursued two incompatible aims: "1. Washington wanted France to fight the anti-Communist war and win, preferably with U.S. guidance and advice; and 2. Washington expected the French, when battlefield victory was assured, to magnanimously withdraw from Indochina."[30] French policy suffered no such incompatibilities; its sole aim was to reassert French power in Indochina. Thus, during the first Indochina War, French and American policy differed in basic purposes.

The United States was compelled to channel its aid to the Bao Dai government through the French because of the emperor's weakness and French insistence. Jealous of their prerogatives in Vietnam and suspicious of American intentions, the French maintained a free hand in the employment of all military and economic aid. Hence, the United States Military Advisory Assistance Group (MAAG) headed in 1954 by Lieutenant General John Wilson (Iron Mike) O'Daniel, was peripheral in importance.

American officials realized that it was necessary to counter Ho Chi Minh's nationalist appeal in order to defeat him; hence they tried to convince the French to give more authority to the Bao Dai regime. The French easily resisted United States pressure in this regard; an ultimate threat at their disposal was to withdraw from Indochina altogether. American policy at this time was dictated by events outside of Vietnam—in Korea and Europe. United States participation in Korea and the turmoil it produced in America precluded a similar action in Vietnam except, possibly, in the event of direct Chinese participation. Hence support for the French in Indochina was the only alternative to a Communist victory there. Unwilling to fight the Viet Minh itself, the United States could not countenance a French withdrawal and subsequent Communist takeover.[31] Furthermore, in the early 1950s American policy makers sought increased French participation in the Atlantic Alliance as well as French receptivity to German rearmament. In the hopes that France would ratify the treaty establishing the European Defense Community (EDC), American officials avoided actions that might incur the wrath of the French National Assembly. Thus, American officials were compelled to support the French effort in Indochina on France's terms.

This support did not resolve the basic ambiguity in United States policy and its disagreement with French policy. The two countries agreed only on the necessity to win the military struggle, not on the purposes for which victory was sought nor on the consequences for French rule after the war was over. As the Defense Department analysts state: "The fact that the American and French means—pushing for military victory—converged in 1950-1954 obscured the fact that the ends of the two nations were inherently incompatible."[32] This disparity between French and American policy became obvious in the context of the Geneva negotiations.

GENEVA 1954

THE NEGOTIATIONS

In late 1953, there were indications that both the French and the Vietnamese wanted negotiations. On November 29, 1953, the *Stockholm*

Expressen carried an exchange of telegrams between its editor and Ho Chi Minh in which the latter mentioned a willingness to seek a solution of the Vietnamese conflict by negotiations. Ho's interest in peace talks was shared reluctantly by the French who had concluded that military victory was impossible. At their insistence, and over American objections, the Indochina question was placed on the agenda of the 1954 Geneva conference which was to discuss Korea.[33]

The conference discussed Indochina from April to July 1954,[34] and throughout the negotiations, the divergence between French and American policy was pronounced. The two countries differed on three essential points: the purpose of the negotiations, the possibility of American military intervention in Indochina, and the United States diplomatic role at the conference.

The Purpose of the Negotiations

Under pressure from political opinion at home and adverse military developments in Vietnam, Premier Joseph Laniel's government was committed to negotiations as the only viable option. Especially after the French defeat at Dien Bien Phu on May 8, 1954, Laniel and his successor, Pierre Mendès-France, were determined to secure the best solution available at the conference table.

In contrast, the United States wanted negotiations only after the French had secured a favorable military position. American policy sought to avoid a French withdrawal on terms that would constitute surrender to the Communists. Reflecting on their own experiences in negotiating with the Communists over the Korean issue at Panmunjum, American officials believed that concessions from them could be won only on the battlefield, not at the conference table. In accord with this estimate, the United States stiffened its opposition to the negotiations as the military situation worsened for the French. Thus the allies drew further apart.

The Possibility of American Military Intervention

Immediately prior to and during the negotiations, the military situation declined seriously for the French. This prompted discussion of possible American military intervention—either unilaterally or as part of an international force. The French, seeking to forestall imminent military defeat, argued for a quick, unilateral American military strike on behalf of their beseiged forces at Dien Bien Phu. They were extremely wary of any wider action. The United States, on the other hand, sought to deny the Communists control in Vietnam permanently by instituting a multi-lateral action, involving troops of its allies in Europe and Asia, which would internationalize the conflict. This came to be known as the "united action" plan.

United States feasibility studies regarding the advisability and timing of American intervention in Indochina began early in 1954. In a March 29 speech, Secretary of State John Foster Dulles raised the possibility of united action in Vietnam. This course seemed preferable to unilateral American intervention because it would avoid the large-scale commitment of American ground troops that might seem unacceptable both to the American public and to international oninion.

Nevertheless, the chairman of the Joint Chiefs of Staff, Admiral Arthur W. Radford, conceived a plan for a unilateral American strike at Dien Bien Phu. Operation Vulture, as the plan was called, consisted of an air strike against Viet Minh artillery positions on the hills surrounding Dien Bien Phu; only through destruction of these sites, from which the Viet Minh was gradually cutting the French off from supplies and reinforcements, could the fortress be saved.

The process by which the American government opted for united action instead of the Radford plan was accelerated by a meeting which Secretary of State Dulles held with members of Congress on April 3, 1954. An account of this meeting by *Washington Post* columnist Chalmers Roberts appeared in the September 14, 1954, issue of the *Reporter*. Roberts maintained that President Eisenhower and Secretary Dulles sought a joint congressional resolution that would permit the use of American air and naval power in Indochina. Reportedly, Dulles had a copy of such a resolution in his pocket during the meeting. However, after Admiral Radford presented his plan for an air strike in relief of Dien Bien Phu, the congressmen, led by minority leader Lyndon B. Johnson, insisted that Dulles first seek the agreement of allied nations who would be willing to participate in a joint operation. Thus, the meeting began an intensive three-week effort by the administration to head off disaster in Indochina by seeking allied approval of a joint strike.[35]

This version of the meeting, its purpose, and its aftermath has been challenged in a study by Robert F. Randle. Randle maintains that neither President Eisenhower nor Secretary Dulles wanted a joint congressional resolution at that time and that Eisenhower's absence from the meeting is significant in this regard. Presumably, if the president had wanted to convince Congress of the necessity of the resolution, he would have come in person. In fact, Randle argues, neither Eisenhower nor Dulles approved of Radford's plan and they called the congressional leaders' meeting to engineer an excuse to veto those activists in the administration, including Vice-President Richard Nixon, who favored the action. In his view, Congress did not impose conditions and did not determine national policy on this issue.[36]

Randle's argument, highly favorable to Dulles throughout, maintains that the secretary sought predictable congressional reactions to the Radford plan to bolster his previously formulated intention to seek allied approval for an intervention. Subsequent United States policy is presented in this account as prudent, cautious, and consistent. In contrast, Roberts concludes that Dulles' own preference for action was inhibited by congressional restraints and that America's pre-Geneva policy was a frantic effort to secure the allied approval that would make intervention possible. Randle's version, equally plausible from the available data, is not necessarily more definitive. However, it is interesting because of its emphasis on the domestic pressures that influenced Dulles, Bidault, and Eden during their pre-Geneva quarrels and made united action, either military or diplomatic, impossible to achieve.[37]

Whatever history's verdict on the wisdom of Mr. Dulles, his policies in the spring and summer of 1954 appeared, in French eyes, to perpetuate the contradictions that had characterized United States actions in Indochina since 1940. The plan for an American strike at Dien Bien Phu was conceived by Admiral Radford and presented to his rather startled French counterpart, General Paul Ely, who visited Washington in late March 1954. The French favored the plan and repeatedly sought to have it activated, particularly as the situation at Dien Bien Phu deteriorated. Instead, the American proposal was modified to provide for the cooperation of several allied countries in a collective venture.

Naturally, the French suspected that the United States was once again pursuing a policy contrary to French interests. They favored swift, unilateral American intervention to improve their immediate military position, but disapproved of multilateral action that might prolong the war and would inevitably dilute their authority in Indochina.

The French were very disappointed when the United States abandoned the idea of a unilateral air strike at Dien Bien Phu. They had been led to believe that the United States supported them militarily but "at the moment when this support was needed, the United States had neither the means nor the will to enter into the combat."[38] Once again, they felt betrayed.

In May 1954, after the fall of Dien Bien Phu, the possibility was again raised of American military intervention in support of the French forces in Indochina. Discussions between France and the United States proceeded into June, but agreement on the terms of intervention was not reached. In particular, the United States specified seven conditions that would have to be met by the French before American intervention would take place. Most odious among these were the requirements that the French Parliament approve a formal request for American military aid and that the states of Indochina be allowed to leave the French Union. The demand for a parliamentary request for military aid was problematic because such a request seemed to contradict the French policy of seeking a diplomatic settlement at Geneva. The demand that the Indochinese states be granted independence was unacceptable, because their preservation in the French Union was the very objective for which the French fought. Thus, the American position was at odds with French political realities and with French policy in Indochina.[39]

The United States Diplomatic Role at Geneva

Finally, the United States and France disagreed on what role the United States was to play at Geneva. Failing a direct military intervention, the French wanted diplomatic support for their position at Geneva. They hoped to use the threat of United States intervention at the conference table and, in addition, to present a firm Western front to enforce the settlement. In contrast to this French position, the United States sought to disengage itself from the negotiating process and to reserve its future options.

Furthermore, American policy looked beyond the immediate situation toward a long-term defense arrangement for Southeast Asia. The united action proposal became the framework from which the Southeast Asia Treaty Organization emerged. As early as April 30, 1954, when Secretary of State Dulles left Geneva, leaving the American delegation in the hands of undersecretary Walter Bedell Smith, he told French Ambassador Chauvel: "We must get that pact."[40] Hence, the United States was already planning for a collective defense treaty for Southeast Asia regardless of the outcome of the Geneva talks. Furthermore, American ambiguity hindered French efforts to threaten the Viet Minh with possible American intervention in Vietnam. Three days after Dien Bien Phu fell, Dulles suggested publicly that Southeast Asia could be defended without Indochina. Bereft of his final bargaining point, the threat of American intervention, French Foreign Minister Bidault "sensed that the backbone of his case had collapsed and his position had become untenable. He was heard to mutter something about a 'stab in the back'."[41]

Indeed, the American delegation at Geneva sought to keep itself at some distance from the deliberations. For example, in Geneva on April 25, Secretary of State Dulles threatened that if highly disadvantageous solutions were proposed, "(we) . . . would probably want to disassociate ourselves from the Conference."[42] On May 10, Bedell Smith underlined the United States position as an unobligated observer of the talks; he rejected Bidault's call that all conference delegations agree in advance to be guarantors of the Geneva settlement.[43]

Dulles' absence from Geneva underlined his resolve to avoid participation in the conference and to maintain distance from an accord which the United States might regard as unsatisfactory. Dulles' deputy, Bedell Smith, was recalled in late June 1954 in line with this stance. The French believed that their position at the conference was weakened by this lack of high level American support. Therefore, Premier Mendès-France argued strongly for the return of either Dulles or Smith. The latter did return to Geneva on July 17, 1954, but only after Mendès-France agreed to a memorandum outlining American and British thoughts regarding an acceptable settlement. Far from a supportive role to French diplomacy at Geneva, the United States held itself at arm's length from the conference and limited France's options. The difficult task of negotiating a favorable settlement was complicated for the French by this American posture.

THE GENEVA ACCORDS

Since both the French and the Viet Minh forces held substantial segments of Vietnamese territory, it became clear that the only solution possible was one based on partition. The French government resisted this course and, at first, refused to negotiate directly with the Viet Minh delegation at Geneva headed by Pham Van Dong. The French hoped to achieve a cease-fire, which would postpone a final political settlement and, toward that end, participated in secret informal negotiations with the Viet Minh. Nevertheless, the Geneva conference was stalemated for two months.

Failure to arrange a settlement brought down the government of Premier Joseph Laniel and, on June 18, 1954, Pierre Mendès-France assumed the premiership of France. One of the earliest and most vocal critics of the Indochina war, Mendès-France had declared the impossibility of a military victory in October 1950; in 1954 he led that group of French parliamentarians who advocated direct negotiations with the Viet Minh. The new premier promised Parliament that he would personally go to Geneva and conclude peace by midnight July 20, 1954, or resign. Arriving in Geneva on June 24, 1954, he gave official status to the ongoing secret truce talks and agreed that the search for an armistice would proceed on the basis of a provisional division of Vietnam. His willingness to negotiate on this basis directly with France's adversaries and the approach of his self-imposed deadline hastened the conclusion of an agreement.

The Geneva accords were concluded in a marathon session of the conference held during the night of July 20-21, 1954, so that Mendès-France might meet his deadline. They consisted of separate truce agreements for Laos, Cambodia, and Vietnam, which were signed by the French and Viet Minh authorities with the acquiescence of the Laotian and Cambodian delegates, and a final declaration, which was submitted to all the conference participants. Vietnam was provisionally divided at the seventeenth parallel, a compromise between the original French demand for the eighteenth and the Viet Minh preference for the thirteenth; the forces of each side were to repair to their respective zones. A demilitarized area was to separate the two zones, and the agreement forbade the introduction of new arms or war material or the establishment of foreign military bases in either zone. The International Commission for Supervision and Control (sometimes referred to as the ICC) composed of Canada, India, and Poland was set up to supervise observation of the truces.[44]

In addition to the truce agreements, the Geneva accords included a final declaration that was assented to orally by all the delegations present at Geneva except that of the United States and South Vietnam. This declaration contained the outlines of a Vietnamese political settlement; in particular, it provided that the boundary at the seventeenth parallel was provisional and that elections to unify Vietnam should be held by secret ballot under the ICC's control within two years after the accords were signed.

The Geneva conferees were faced with the impossible task of reconciling conflicting national viewpoints on a complicated series of problems. After months of discussions, the maximum area of common agreement remained narrow so that the resulting accords tended to obfuscate the issues. Beyond the French-Viet Minh cease-fire, there was little upon which the delegates could agree. Unfortunately, the absence of agreement regarding the terms of the final political settlement and the procedures for its implementation necessitated a series of provisions that proved incomplete and unenforceable.[45]

Furthermore, the obligations incurred by the delegates were of dubious legality and force since, except for the truce agreements, the accords were unsigned. Assent to the final declaration was given orally by the delegations' chiefs; the participants of the Geneva conference thereby christened "a new form of legal obligation between states—an unsigned treaty."[46] Finally, the accords were handicapped by lack of support from the American and South Vietnamese delegates without whom they could not have been enforced.

FRANCE WITHDRAWS FROM VIETNAM

The elections for a government that would unify the two zones of Vietnam, provided for in the Geneva accords, were to be held no later than July 20, 1956. In the interim between 1954 and 1956, the responsibility for maintaining order in Vietnam and for overseeing the faithful execution of the accords rested with the signatories of the 1954 armistice agreement, France, and the Democratic Republic of (North) Vietnam. However, the French did not insist on their prerogatives and, instead, turned over political power in the southern sector to the regime headed by Ngo Dinh Diem.[47] The latter, supported by the United States, refused even to discuss the proposed elections with the Hanoi government. Three months before the July 20, 1956, deadline, the French expeditionary force had completely withdrawn from Vietnam, so that France no longer possessed the means to interfere forceably in Vietnamese affairs. Hence, France was powerless to oppose Ngo Dinh Diem when he refused to honor the election provision in the 1954 agreement. In fact, by allowing Diem full power under American tutelage, France abdicated its responsibilities under the Geneva accords and cooperated in the introduction of American military power into the Vietnamese equation.

Naturally, the events of 1954-56 exacerbated French-American hostility regarding Vietnam. After the 1954 accords the United States rapidly moved to supplant French influence in Vietnam. By September 1954, "U.S. policy began to respond to military urgency, and this in turn caused the U.S. to move beyond partnership [with France] to primacy."[48] After that time, the United States dealt directly with the Saigon government and not through France as before. On October 23, 1954, President Eisenhower wrote to Premier Diem offering him American support; this letter was subsequently referred to by President Johnson as the beginning of the American commitment to defend South Vietnam.

The French resented these American actions which they believed to be misguided and detrimental to French interests. American sustenance strengthened a South Vietnamese regime which was unstable domestically and whose foreign policy was violently anti-French. President Eisenhower's letter to Premier Diem was viewed in France as directed against French interests.[49] Furthermore, arrangements for the transfer from French to American military advisers of the function of training the South Vietnamese army were delayed because of the misgivings of the French government. An agreement on this point was concluded between General Paul Ely, French commander in Vietnam, and General Lawton Collins, head of a special United States mission to Vietnam (November 1954 to May 1955), on December 13, 1954, but was not accepted by the French government until February 11, 1955. The delay in France's acceptance of this transferral agreement indicates the reluctance with which the French officials saw their functions assumed by the Americans. By April 1956, French troops had completely withdrawn from Vietnam, and French influence had been eclipsed by that of the United States. The loss of their colonial status in Indochina was made more difficult for the French by the installation in their place of an American protectorate.

Clearly, during the years 1954-56 France and the United States perceived their interests in Southeast Asia quite differently and pursued their policies accordingly. Chief among the points of discord was their attitude toward the Geneva accords and toward the regime of Ngo Dinh Diem.

United States policy was based on the premise that the Geneva accords were, in the words of Defense Department analysts, "a disaster," and that the French defeat required that the United States assume defense of the free world's interests in Southeast Asia. In the period immediately following the 1954 conference, the United States sought to minimize further

Communist gains in Asia. This was the purpose of the defense pact signed
at Manila on September 8, 1954, which created the Southeast Asia Treaty
Organization (SEATO). Secretary of State Dulles advocated that the
three Indochinese states of Laos, Cambodia, and Vietnam become members of SEATO to the consternation of the French delegation at Manila.[50]
Reminded by the French that Article 19 of the Geneva armistice agreement forbade the Indochinese states from entering military alliances, the
United States instead inserted a protocol to the treaty that included the
Indochinese states in the area to be protected by the alliance without
having them actually join. This created a curious modification of the
principle of collective defense in which three states were to be protected
by the signatories but not themselves bound by the treaty. Though the
arrangement did not technically violate the Geneva agreement, it indicated lack of respect for the goal of the Geneva negotiators, namely,
that Indochina be neutralized or freed from further military intervention
by outside powers. Subsequently, Cambodia (unilaterally in 1955) and
Laos (by international agreement in 1962) rejected their inclusion in the
SEATO protocol.

A further element of American policy in the years immediately following Geneva was its support of the government of Ngo Dinh Diem. The
United States believed that there was no alternative to the Diem government if South Vietnam was to remain non-Communist. American policy
makers entirely concurred in Diem's decision not to hold the 1956 elections lest Ho Chi Minh emerge victorious.[51]

Unqualified support for Diem was another indication of United States
disregard for the Geneva accords. Although the American delegate at
Geneva promised that the United States would refrain from disrupting
the accords, subsequent American actions indicated the insincerity of
this pledge. On the contrary, if application of the election provision
abandoned Vietnam to Communism, the United States was opposed
to implementing the accords. The Geneva settlement was useful from the
American perspective only insofar as it kept South Vietnam independent
and non-Communist—something it was not designed to accomplish. If
the Geneva framework subverted this purpose, it was to be ignored.

In contrast, French policy from 1954 to 1956 favored application of
the Geneva accords. The French regarded the 1954 agreement as the best
that could be obtained under bad circumstances. In the aftermath, they
hoped to safeguard their economic interests and to retain some of their

political influence in Indochina. However, they were resolved to avoid
further military involvement there.

It can be argued that French interests would have been served had the
Geneva accords been executed; the Geneva framework permitted a French
role in Vietnam, at least until 1956.[52] Both the extreme Right and the
extreme Left in French politics favored a policy that maximized French
gains in the post-Geneva situation. Hence, "had the Geneva Settlement
been fulfilled, France might have retained a presence and influence in
Vietnam that would have mollified both the Right and Left."[53] Instead,
French influence was replaced by that of the United States.

Although the French agreed with the United States on the desirability
of preserving a pro-Western regime in South Vietnam, they were much
more pessimistic than the Americans about Diem's ability to survive.
Clearly, their negative assessment of Diem reflected his hostility to France
as well as his increasing reliance on the United States. Nevertheless, the
French could claim some expertise in the area of South Vietnamese politics, and they believed that Diem's leadership was hopelessly inept. Furthermore, Diem had denounced the Geneva accords and had indicated
his unwillingness to abide by their provisions. Thus, the French had some
cause to seek alternatives to the Diem government.

Throughout the fall of 1954 and the winter of 1955, opposition to
Diem was mounting among Vietnamese in Saigon and in France. The latter
included the Emperor Bao Dai who still held the office of South Vietnamese president. The French encouraged Bao Dai's attempts to retain his
power and to name another premier in Diem's place, and they sought to
convince the United States that Diem must go. However, the French refused to use their remaining military forces in South Vietnam to overthrow the Diem regime. The French commander, General Ely, was convinced that Diem had to be replaced but, on orders from Paris, he refused
to intervene forceably. Instead he followed a course which he described
to his deputy, Jean Daridan, in the following words: "we must support
Diem until the moment when the Americans understand that they must
get rid of him."[54]

In the months after the Geneva agreement, the French tried unsuccess-
fully to convince the United States to replace Diem. Finally, on April 27,
1955, Secretary of State Dulles agreed to consider a change in the Saigon
government and so informed the American embassy in Saigon. At this
critical juncture, Diem moved forceably to subdue his opponents in Sai-

gon. His success prompted the United States to reaffirm its support, and the Saigon embassy quietly burned the April 27 telegram. It is notable that General Ely, who commanded 75,000 troops in South Vietnam as of April 1955 did not intervene in favor of Diem's opponents. To have done so, he knew, would have incurred American wrath.[55]

A French-American-British foreign ministers' meeting in Paris in May 1955 was climactic. When Southeast Asia was discussed, the sharp differences between France and the United States became apparent. Both sides professed their willingness to withdraw entirely from Vietnam rather than risk straining their alliance with each other. However, it was the French who withdrew whereas, shortly after the May 1955 meeting, the American secretary of state indicated clearly the United States intent to act independently of France regarding Vietnam.

Saying the problem in Vietnam did not lend itself to a contractual agreement between France and the United States, Dulles suggested each should state its policy and proceed accordingly. In effect, said Dulles, the days of joint policy are over, the U.S. will act (more) independently of France in the future.[56]

Thus, less than one year after the Geneva accords were signed, the United States asserted its intent to conduct a forceful Vietnam policy divorced from that of France.

In spite of French hostility to American aims, France was the reluctant partner to United States policy in Vietnam from 1954 to 1956. The French did not fulfill their obligation to see that the various provisions of the Geneva agreements were implemented; instead, they turned power over to Diem, whose dependence on the United States was apparent. Furthermore, transferral by France of its advisory functions in Vietnam to the American military violated the spirit if not the letter of the Geneva prohibition against the introduction of outside forces into either zone of Vietnam. Thus the French acquiesced in an American policy which ignored the accords they had so recently negotiated. There were several compelling reasons for France's actions.

First, the French were limited in the options available to them. Enforcing a policy distinct from that of the United States would have required resources which the French did not possess. They were unable to risk further armed involvement in Vietnam; no significant element of

French politics or the French public would have favored such a course. Furthermore, even the support of remaining French garrisons in Indochina required American funds. Hence, French policy was necessarily dependent on that of the United States.

After the Geneva settlement, the French initially hoped to maintain good relations with both Vietnamese regimes. A French mission headed by Jean Sainteny, Ho Chi Minh's old collaborator, was dispatched to Hanoi in August 1954 to work out a *modus vivendi* between France and North Vietnam. In the South, the French hoped that the Diem regime might be replaced by a government less hostile to France; however, this possibility became less likely as relations between Saigon and Washington solidified. Furthermore, the xenophobic Diem regime was suspicious of France's approach to the North Vietnamese, and under pressure from Saigon and Washington, the French severely restricted the scope of the Sainteny mission. Hanoi could hardly have approved of French policy which ignored the Geneva accords and established the American advisory role to the Saigon regime. Thus, the French had to choose between the two Vietnamese regimes; in view of French dependence on the United States, there was no question what that choice would be.

Second, the French were hampered in working out a coherent policy regarding Vietnam after their military involvement by the chronic political instability that characterized the Fourth Republic. Their attitude toward Diem is a good example. The regime of Premier Joseph Laniel and Foreign Minister Georges Bidault was in power when France installed Diem as head of the South Vietnamese government. They were much more supportive of Diem than was Pierre Mendès-France, who took over the French government two days after Diem became South Vietnam's premier. Mèndes-France was succeeded late in February 1955 by the Socialist Edgar Faure and the latter, new in office, was ill-equipped to handle the difficulties that erupted in South Vietnam in April of that year.

Third, the French were preoccupied with other problems. In November 1954, a revolt broke out in Algeria that required the attention of French politicians and the French army. French prestige was at stake in the Algerian war, and military and political leaders were determined not to fail. In contrast, the Indochina war was already lost and best forgotten. This partially explains France's willingness to terminate its responsibilities in Indochina.

Finally, the French could not risk alienating the United States. The

Geneva settlement meant that France accepted the end of its privileged
role in Indochina, and subsequently, the French had no choice but to
acquiesce in a series of developments that led to increased American involvement there. In fact, the French were at pains to demonstrate that
they were loyal and competent allies in the wake of their failure in Indochina and of the defeat by the French Assembly of the European Defense
Community (EDC) in August 1954. The latter action was graver because
it affected the European alliance, which was paramount to both the United
States and France. Pierre Mendès-France, premier of France when the
EDC was defeated, had refused to make the matter an issue of confidence
in his government. Thus, it was crucial that he demonstrate to the United
States France's solidarity and his own anti-Communism; he did so by
supporting SEATO and by cooperating with United States policy toward
Indochina in late 1954.[57]

During the 1954-56 period both France and the United States insisted
that their relationship with each other was too important to be jeopardized
by differences over Indochina; nevertheless, events in Vietnam increased
the hostility between the two allies. In the words of the Pentagon analysts:

the whole episode of French withdrawal from Vietnam, in fact, soured
the Western alliance. . . . American policy in the aftermath of Geneva
widely alienated affection for the U.S. in France, and created that lack
of confidence which the Suez crisis of summer 1956 translated into out-
right distrust.[58]

The French learned several lessons as a result of their war in Indochina.
After their futile struggle with the Viet Minh, they appreciated the diffi-
culty of opposing efforts of national resistance set in motion as a result
of World War II; they emerged with a healthy respect for their Viet Minh
opponents. Furthermore, France was forced to accept limits on its global
domain; for a country to whom empire was the corollary of great power
status, the loss of Indochina was a clear indication of France's reduced
rank after World War II. The French did not easily accept this fact; only
after the 1956 Suez crisis and Algerian independence in 1962 did France
definitively reject empire. Finally, the Indochina war left French leaders
bitter over American policy. France reproached the United States for
Roosevelt's initial opposition to the reassertion of French control in

Indochina after World War II, for its subsequent grudging admission that the area lay in the French domain, for its lukewarm diplomatic support during the 1954 Geneva conference, and for its readiness to assume France's place in Vietnam immediately after Geneva. The French believed that the United States had undercut their position in Vietnam and had made them accomplices to the insertion of American military power there. Their bitterness was aggravated by their own inability to frustrate these developments. The first Indochina war left French officials with the clear impression that United States interests in Vietnam after 1940 had been furthered at France's expense. They believed that United States policy opposed the maintenance of French influence in Southeast Asia. France's attitude toward future American military involvement in Vietnam was rooted in the resentment of this earlier period.

NOTES

1. Throughout this chapter, unless otherwise specified, the words "Indochina" and "Vietnam" are used interchangeably. Prior to the development of semi-autonomous governments in Laos and Cambodia as well as two rival Vietnamese regimes, the area was commonly referred to as Indochina. However, even in the early post-World War II period, the source of French-American discord was the area more correctly called "Vietnam."

2. "Federation" and "community" were vague terms whose meaning in 1945 was far from clear. However, since the federation would be composed of five parties—the three provinces of Vietnam (Tonkin, Annam, and Cochinchina) plus Laos and Cambodia—it entailed continuation of the divide-and-rule policy by which French control over Vietnam had been perpetuated. Therefore the Vietnamese, who favored union of the three provinces of Vietnam in an independent entity, opposed the French idea.

3. An account of Ho's activities in China appears in King C. Chen, *Vietnam and China 1938-1954* (Princeton: Princeton University Press, 1969), Ch. 2.

4. Charles de Gaulle, *The War Memoirs of Charles de Gaulle,* vol. 3, *Salvation 1944-1946* (New York: Simon and Schuster, 1960), p. 262.

5. The following discussion is based partly on Georges Chaffard's account of these events in *Les deux guerres du Vietnam; de Valluy à Westmoreland* (Paris: La Table Ronde, 1969), pp. 79-80 (note).

6. One reason for French resentment of the Chinese was the actions of the Chinese commander in Hanoi, General Lu Han, who did not agree with his country's neutral policy and was not very respectful of French prerogatives. An account of the Chinese occupation policy appears in Chen, *Vietnam and China* pp. 132-154. For a French account of the difficult French-Chinese relations during this period see Jean Sainteny, *Histoire d'une paix manquée* (Paris: Fayard, 1967), pp. 156-177.

7. In fact, Chiang Kai-shek had supported President Roosevelt's initial inclination to prevent the French from returning to Indochina.

8. Quoted in Chen, *Vietnam and China*, p. 99.

9. Quoted by Sainteny, *Histoire*, p. 199.

10. Ibid.

11. Colonel Debes' decision to use force was in line with the wishes of his superiors from French Premier Georges Bidault on down. The French military commander for Asia, General Valluy, instructed Debes by telegram on November 22, 1946, as follows: "By all the means at your disposal, you should extend your authority completely over Haiphong and bring the Vietnamese government and army to repentance." Chaffard, *Les deux guerres*, p. 44. Furthermore, in addition to his military authority, General Valluy was temporarily replacing the chief French political authority in Indochina, Admiral Thierry d'Argenlieu, who concurred with using force against the Vietnamese.

12. General Morliere, a moderate who was the military commander in Tonkin and Debes' immediate superior, quoted in Chaffard, *Les deux guerres*, p. 58. Morliere's harsh judgment of Debes reflects their disagreements regarding the use of force in Vietnam in late 1946. Morliere's dissatisfaction with official French policy in this regard caused him to be relieved of his Vietnamese command early in 1947.

13. The switch from Gouin to Bidault took place at the moment the Vietnamese delegation, headed by Ho Chi Minh and Pham Van Dong, arrived in France for the Fontainebleu talks. The delegates had to wait several weeks in Biarritz before proceeding to Paris where the newly organized French government belatedly welcomed them. This indication of France's governmental instability was not an auspicious beginning for the conference.

14. The resilient Bao Dai was summoned in turn by the Japanese in March 1945, by the Viet Minh in August 1945, and by the French in June 1949 to provide the governments each sponsored with a symbol of continuity with Vietnam's past.

15. Phillippe Devillers and Jean Lacouture, *End of a War; Indochina 1954*, trans. Alexander Lieven and Adam Roberts (New York: Praeger, 1969), p. 19. This theme is reinforced by R.E.M. Irving, *The First Indochina War* (London: Crown Helm, 1975), a study of French political parties and Indochina policy 1945-54. For a discussion of the French Left and Vietnam, see Ellen J. Hammer, *The Struggle for Indochina* (Stanford, Calif.: Stanford University Press, 1954), pp. 230-300.

16. Bernard Fall, *Street without Joy* (Harrisburg, Pa.: Telegraphic Press, 1961), p. 23. See also his "La Politique Americaine au Viet-Nam," *Politique Etrangere* 20, no. 3 (June-July 1955), pp. 299-322.

17. Cordell Hull, *Memoirs*, vol. 2 (New York: Macmillan, 1948), p. 1957. An account of Roosevelt's discussions of Indochina with Stalin at Teheran (November-December 1943) appears in Charles E. Bohlen, *Witness to History, 1929-1969* (New York: W. W. Norton, 1973), p. 140. Stalin was not altogether in agreement with Roosevelt's idea that Indochina should be taken from France, according to Bohlen, who served as an interpreter at the conference.

18. American assurances to this effect were contained in the following communications: "August 2, 1941, official statement on the French-Japanese agree-

ment; a December 1941 presidential letter to Pétain; a March 2, 1942, statement on New Caledonia; a note to the French ambassador of April 13, 1942; presidential statements and messages at the time of the North Africa invasion; the Clark-Darlan Agreement of November 22, 1942; and a letter of the same month from the president's personal representative to General Henri Giraud." *United States-Vietnam Relations 1945-1967; Study Prepared by the Department of Defense* (Washington, D.C.: U.S. Government Printing Office, 1971), Book I, Part I.A, p. A-13. (This version of the Pentagon Papers was released by the House Committee on Armed Services.)

19. *The War Memoirs of Charles de Gaulle*, vol. 3, *Salvation*, p. 190.

20. Ibid., pp. 243-261.

21. Sainteny writes that Chennault himself understood the French position and recommended that aiding France would be in the allied cause. *Histoire*, pp. 34-35.

22. Interview with Jean Sainteny, Paris, July 6, 1973.

23. The title of a chapter in his book.

24. Sainteny, *Histoire*, p. 86.

25. OSS contacts with Ho are discussed in *Hearings on Causes, Origins and Lessons of the Vietnam War, May 9, 10, and 11, 1972*, U.S. Senate, Committee on Foreign Relations, pp. 241-340.

26. Actually, the United States ignored Ho Chi Minh's several appeals in 1945 and 1946 to internationalize the Vietnamese issue, and instead, American policy acquiesced in the French return to Indochina.

27. For a discussion of the evolution of Roosevelt's attitude toward Indochina, see Walter La Feber, "Roosevelt, Churchill, and Indochina: 1942-45," *American Historical Review*, 80 (December 1975), pp. 1277-1295.

28. *United States-Vietnam Relations*, Book I, Part I.A, p. A-20. (Emphasis added.) Another factor which influenced the American decision was American concern to retain freedom of action concerning the fate of the Pacific Islands which the United States had captured from the Japanese.

29. *United States-Vietnam Relations*, Book I, Part I.A, p. A-5.

30. Ibid., Book I, Part II.A, p. A-2.

31. Ibid., pp. A-38-39.

32. Ibid., p. A-41.

33. The pessimism of French leaders concerning the war spread to the French public whose support for the war had been based on the goal of retaining Vietnam as a French colony. According to former Ambassador Jean Chauvel (who headed France's permanent delegation to the 1954 Geneva conference), the French were not fighting to keep Indochina non-Communist; if they could not keep it in the French Union, they wanted out of the war. Interview with Ambassador Jean Chauvel, Paris, June 20, 1972.

34. The participants were Soviet Union, China, France, United Kingdom, United States, Cambodia, Laos, Democratic Republic of Vietnam (Viet Minh), and Republic of Vietnam (Bao Dai's government). Neither the Pathet Lao nor the Khmer Rouge delegations were recognized. For an interesting profile of the conference participants, see Devillers and Lacouture, *End of a War*, Ch. 8.

35. Chalmers M. Roberts, "The Day We Didn't Go to War," *The Reporter*,

September 14, 1954; reprinted in Wesley R. Fishel, ed., *Vietnam: Anatomy of a Conflict* (Itasca, Ill.: F. E. Peacock Publishers, Inc., 1968), pp. 29-32.

36. Robert F. Randle, *Geneva 1954: The Settlement of the Indochina War* (Princeton: Princeton University Press, 1969), pp. 63-64, 118-119.

37. In particular, Randle emphasizes the connection between the EDC treaty and the Indochinese negotiations. Ibid., p. 42. The French parliament had not ratified the treaty, and Foreign Minister Bidault threatened to oppose it if Secretary of State Dulles did not agree to place Indochina on the agenda of the Geneva meeting. *United States-Vietnam Relations,* Book I, Part II, pp. A-40-41.

38. Interview with Ambassador Jean Chauvel, Paris, June 20, 1972.

39. *United States-Vietnam Relations,* Book I, Part III.A, pp. A-16-26.

40. Interview with Ambassador Jean Chauvel, Paris, June 20, 1972.

41. Devillers and Lacouture, *End of a War,* p. 189. In his memoirs, Bidault characterized Dulles' Indochina policy as "a policy of many tough words but little action." *Resistance* (New York: Praeger, 1967), p. 201.

42. *United States-Vietnam Relations,* Book I, Part III.A, p. A-8.

43. Ibid., p. A-10.

44. In Laos, the Viet Minh-Pathet Lao troops were to regroup in two northern Laotian provinces prior to an eventual agreement between them and the Royal Laotian government; Cambodia, more fortunately, emerged with its territory intact and free from subversive elements.

45. Bernard Fall, "How the French Got Out of Vietnam," in Fall and Marcus Raskin, eds., *The Vietnam Reader* (New York: Vintage Books, 1967), pp. 81-95. Fall demonstrates how the accords failed politically and economically before they failed militarily.

46. Devillers and Lacouture, *End of a War,* p. 300.

47. Premier Diem had been selected by President Bao Dai as head of South Vietnam's government on June 16, 1954, just two days before Pierre Mendès-France became the sixteenth premier of the Fourth Republic. Bao Dai continued to serve as South Vietnam's chief of state.

48. *United States-Vietnam Relations 1945-1967,* Book I, Part IV. A.3, p. ii.

49. Devillers and Lacouture, *End of a War,* p. 295, and Jacques Vernant, "Les Etats-Unis et l'Asie du Sud-Est," *Revue de Défense Nationale,* 20 (April 1964), pp. 706-711.

50. The signatories of the SEATO treaty were Australia, France, New Zealand, Pakistan, the Phillippines, Thailand, the United States, and the United Kingdom. The head of the French delegation to the Manila conference which approved the treaty, Ambassador Jean Chauvel, expressed particular concern because SEATO was signed before the 300 days provided for by the Geneva accords for the regroupment of French and Vietnamese troops had been completed. Prior to this regroupment, any direct violation of the accords might have caused the resumption of hostilities. Interview with Ambassador Jean Chauvel, Paris, June 20, 1972.

51. Franklin B. Weinstein, *Vietnam's Unheld Elections: The Failure to Carry Out the 1956 Reunification Elections and the Effect on Hanoi's Present Outlook,*

Data Paper No. 60, Southeast Asia Program, Cornell University, Ithaca, N.Y.,
July 1966.

52. All of the governments present at Geneva—with the notable exception of
South Vietnam's—expected France to remain in Vietnam. *United States-Vietnam
Relations 1945-1967*, Book I, Part IV A.3, p. ii.

53. Ibid., p. i.

54. Quoted by Georges Chaffard from Daridan's account to him. *Les deux
guerres*, p. 183.

55. Paul Ely, *Memoires: Indochine dans la Tourmente* (Paris: Plon, 1964),
pp. 318-319.

56. *United States-Vietnam Relations 1945-1967*, Book I, Part IV A.3, p. 37.

57. Chaffard, *Les deux guerres*, pp. 180-181.

58. *United States-Vietnam Relations 1945-1967*, Book I, Part IV A.3, p. ii.

Chapter 3

The Fifth Republic
and Vietnam

President Charles de Gaulle's public criticism of direct American involvement in the Vietnam war is examined in the next chapter. Here, some factors that underlay the Gaullist critique will be set forth. First, there were two instances early in the Fifth Republic (which began in 1958) and prior to substantial United States troop participation in the war that illustrated continuing French-American differences regarding Vietnam: the crises in Laos from 1960 to 1962 and the events preceding the overthrow of Ngo Dinh Diem in 1963. Second, it is instructive to examine de Gaulle's genuine conviction that United States policy in Vietnam did not suit the circumstances there; his interpretation of events in Vietnam, diametrically opposed to that of the United States, was an essential cause of his criticism of American policy. Last, the Gaullist critique of United States actions in Vietnam was delivered against the background of strong support within France for de Gaulle's analysis of the Vietnam situation.

DIFFERING FRENCH-AMERICAN PERSPECTIVES REGARDING LAOS

The crises that Laos experienced from 1960 to 1962 provided an issue over which French-American differences regarding Indochina were manifest. The Fifth Republic was as apprehensive as its predecessor regarding United States policy in Southeast Asia. In Laos, as elsewhere in Indochina, American influence exemplified by American aid and advisory personnel had replaced that of France after 1954. Ironically, it was through the French military aid mission that some of this assistance was funneled in order to uphold the Geneva accords' prohibition against foreign (non-French) military personnel. Nevertheless, there were more Americans in Laos in 1961 than there were Frenchmen there in 1940. From 1954 onward, personnel from various American governmental agencies, who sometimes worked at cross-purposes with each other, participated in military instruction, political organization, and economic assistance.[1] They sought to interfere in the complicated struggles between various nationalist, neutralist, and Pathet Lao factions so that the victors would be pro-Western in orientation.

The French believed that this policy was unrealistic. Although they shared the American desire for a pro-Western government, they were pessimistic about the chances of obtaining one. They knew from experience that Laos was militarily indefensible and that Laos' Communist neighbors would not tolerate a strong pro-Western government. Hence, both internal and external factors seemed to warrant some type of neutralist regime in Laos.

The French press echoed governmental pessimism regarding Laos and displayed healthy skepticism toward one-sided accounts of the situation there. French reporters assigned to Laos were less confident of the Laotian government's press releases than most of their American colleagues especially regarding reports of a North Vietnamese "invasion" in the summer of 1959. The American press viewed the French attitude as "either 'sour grapes' or simply as another case of French paranoic anti-Americanism."[2]

French-American differences over Laos surfaced in 1960 when rumors in diplomatic and journalistic circles alleged that France was actively supporting the paratroop commander Kong Le who revolted against the American-sponsored right-wing government. Kong Le recalled to office the neutralist Prince Souvanna Phouma who had been ousted from the premiership in July 1958 as a result of American pressure. The French had some reason to trust Souvanna, whose neutrality was regarded as suspect in Washington. He had cooperated with France in 1949 when he broke away from the rebellion he and two of his half-brothers had been

leading and accepted a compromise by which France granted a measure
of independence to Laos. In 1951 he assumed the premiership of the
Laotian government, attempting to reconcile the warring factions and
cooperating with France in the pre-Geneva period. In the complications
that followed, he was in and out of office spending the period after his
1958 ouster as ambassador to France. He undoubtedly used this opportunity to expound his position to the leaders of the Fifth Republic who
promptly recognized the government he formed after Kong Le's coup.

Subsequently, the right-wing General Phoumi Nosavan initiated full-
scale hostilities forcing Kong Le to align his forces with those of the
Pathet Lao. United States policy makers had dismissed French and
British warnings that the American commitment to Phoumi would un-
happily force the neutralists to cooperate with the Communists. The
Americans seemed to regard this counsel as "tainted with 'British lack of
guts' or 'French colonial intrigue'."[3] Their refusal to acknowledge the
existence of any true neutralists reflected an oversimplified view of the
situation not unlike that with which de Gaulle charged later American
administrations regarding Vietnam. Although de Gaulle refrained from
public criticism of American policy in Laos, the disparity between the
French and American analyses of the situation was obvious.[4]

The reconvened and expanded Geneva conference[5] scheduled to consider the Laotian problem in May 1961 was preceded by discussions
among the Western allies regarding a common position. Throughout
these consultations France and the United States forcefully disagreed,
especially over the question of armed intervention by SEATO forces to
which the French were unalterably opposed. Although objections to intervention and arguments in favor of accepting a truly neutral Laotian government were enunciated with greater force by the French, it was the British
advice along the same lines that prevailed. The hostility that had developed
between France and the United States over Laos since 1954 had left its
residue of tension which, coupled with the anti-French bias of the incom-
ing Kennedy administration, caused American policy makers to doubt
the value of French advice.[6]

Most accounts of the Laotian conference of 1961-62 stress the importance of bilateral Russo-American contacts in achieving agreement on a
settlement. Clearly, President Kennedy and his advisers believed that the
key to a Laotian settlement lay in Moscow, and Laos was about the only
subject on which Kennedy and Krushchev are said to have agreed at their

meeting in Vienna in June 1961. The necessity of cooperation between
the two superpowers to settle a struggle between their distant proxies suggests the limits surrounding action by a middle power, such as France,
in such a situation. In spite of French experience in Indochina and France's
special responsibilities in Laos, it was superpower agreement and pressure
on the combatants that finally brought about the 1962 Laotian settlement.

On the other hand, the French played an important role at the conference. They succeeded in bringing together the two half-brothers who
headed rival Laotian factions, Souvanna Phouma and Souphanouvong.
French Ambassador Jean Chauvel, who permanently headed the French
delegation to the Geneva conference in 1961-62 (as he had in 1954), presented the only major Western proposal to come before the conference.
The French format called for a declaration of neutrality by the government of Laos which would then be seconded by the other thirteen participants of the conference. This formula was accepted in lieu of the Soviet
proposal for a single text whereby all fourteen nations would declare
Laos neutral.

In accepting neutral status, the new tripartite government of Laos explicitly rejected the protection extended to it by the protocols to the
SEATO treaty. This step, together with recognition of Laotian neutrality
by the interested nations and their pledge at Geneva to uphold it, brought
Laos closer to true neutral status than the other states of former French
Indochina. Although the 1954 agreement had specified that Laos, Cambodia, and Vietnam reject foreign alliances and bases in favor of a neutral
stance, the obligations of the "signatories" were vague; the 1962 accords
specifically obligated its adherents to observe Laotian neutrality, the
characteristics of which were defined. In addition, the United States,
which had rather pointedly disassociated itself from the 1954 agreements,
openly adhered to those concluded in 1962.

Convened in the midst of a three-way civil war whose participants
were each sponsored by a major power, the Geneva conference of 1961-
62 maintained the fiction that it dealt merely with the international
aspects of the Laotian question, acknowledging the exclusive right of
the Laotians to settle their own internal difficulties. Leaving aside the
dilemma as to whether a state's international posture can ever be separated from its internal politics, this distinction seems particularly inap-
plicable to Laos in 1961 since the principal business of the delegates at
Geneva was to achieve a cease-fire and an accord among the warring fac-

tions. However, perhaps taking their cue from the ineffectiveness of the
1954 accords, the delegates to the later conference left the details for
internal reconciliation to those who would have to execute them.

General de Gaulle's subsequent statements concerning peace in Vietnam contained elements reminiscent of the 1962 Laotian settlement.
First, he believed that the neutral status of Vietnam and Cambodia should
be distinctly defined and upheld by all interested parties as was that of
Laos in 1962. In his view the defects of the 1954 Geneva agreement
could only be rectified and true neutralization of the Indochinese peninsula established by this approach and so he regarded it as the only basis
for future peace in the area.

Second, he was convinced that an international conference convened
for the purpose of an Indochinese settlement ought to emulate the 1962
meeting and concern itself, as much as possible, with the "international"
aspects of the situation. Although he advocated dealings with all parties
concerned in the struggle for control of South Vietnam (which, in itself
prejudices resolution of the domestic issue somewhat), de Gaulle's approach called for an internal settlement based on agreement among the
contending factions which would then be ratified by the conference. The
fundamental right of the factions involved in Vietnam to settle their own
fate as well as the practicality of this approach was a crucial element in
de Gaulle's estimate of the Vietnamese situation and a fundamental source
of his disagreement with the United States in this matter.

Third, de Gaulle's prescription for a settlement in Vietnam emulated
the 1961-62 conference on Laos in the matter of French participation.
The French delegation introduced the major Western proposal at the
1961-62 conference; it also participated in the crucial work of the "drafting committee" which resolved all the issues unsettled by the plenary sessions. This committee included the United Kingdom, the Soviet Union,
China, India, and France from its inception after July 26, 1961, until
after August 16, 1961, when the United States, Canada, and Poland
joined. Since the key decisions were made by this group which one source
described as "the embodiment of great power influence,"[7] French membership is significant. Finally, France was one of the thirteen nations whose
signature on the accord indicated its pledge to uphold Laotian neutrality.
De Gaulle hoped that French participation in a Vietnamese settlement
could be of equal importance. Unfortunately, his hopes were not realized.[8]

SAIGON 1963

After the 1954 Geneva accords there was residual bitterness between France and the leaders of South Vietnam who resented the partition of their country. Ngo Dinh Diem, who became South Vietnam's premier as the Geneva accords were being concluded, was especially bitter toward the French, some of whom had intrigued against him in the mid-1950s. However, by 1963, relations between France and the Saigon government were improving slightly. The account of France's role in Vietnam during 1963 is instructive in understanding its subsequent attitude vis à vis Saigon's leaders and toward the Washington/Saigon axis.

Ellen Hammer, an authority on Vietnamese affairs described 1963 as "a very exciting time in Saigon, a time of political flux."[9] American-South Vietnamese relations were strained and French ambassador to Saigon, Roger Lalouette, was encouraging Diem to put distance between himself and the United States. Ambassador Lalouette's account of the political crisis which ultimately caused Diem's overthrow and murder emphasizes Diem's concern over the direct involvement of American advisers in Vietnamese affairs. "They come without passports," Diem told Lalouette in the spring of 1963, and, so, I don't know how many there are nor how I can control them."[10] In Lalouette's view, the pattern was the same for all colonial enterprises: "first, you come with advice and then the advisers take over because they think they can run things best."[11] Lalouette advised Diem to "gently" ask that some of the United States advisers leave, and he believed the South Vietnamese leader was receptive to this advice. The Defense Department analysts note that, by 1963, Diem had complained to the United States about the quantity and zeal of American advisers who were "creating a colonial impression among the people."[12] According to the Central Intelligence Agency, tension between the United States and South Vietnam by mid-April 1963 was "considerable."[13] In Lalouette's eyes, Diem was "a patriot above all": as such, he was not anxious to surrender his country to American control after the long fight against French colonialism. Furthermore, Ho Chi Minh seems to have shared this view; he reportedly described Diem in 1963 as "a patriot like me."[14]

Implicit in Diem's turning away from the United States was the possibility that Saigon would seek a peaceful accommodation with Hanoi and that the French might have a role in the rapprochement between

North and South. Ambassador Lalouette was anxious to improve France's relations with South Vietnam, and he encouraged Diem to open contacts with Hanoi. French economic interests in Vietnam would have been well served if American influence were reduced and if the civil conflict was resolved.

Naturally, the United States was suspicious of the feelers which Diem and his brother Nhu, encouraged by the French, were advancing to representatives of the North Vietnamese. Furthermore, American officials were undoubtedly upset by what they must have regarded as Lalouette's meddling at a time when United States-South Vietnamese relations were not entirely cordial.[15]

American dissatisfaction with Diem was apparent in the summer and fall of 1963 when it was decided to seek the removal of Nhu from the South Vietnamese government. In a cable dispatched on August 24, 1963, shortly after he assumed his duties as the new American ambassador to South Vietnam, Henry Cabot Lodge received the following instructions from the State Department:

U.S. Government cannot tolerate situation in which power lies in Nhu's hands. Diem must be given chance to rid himself of Nhu and his coterie and replace them with best military and political personalities available.[16]

Furthermore, the Kennedy administration was prepared to deal with the possibility that Diem would refuse to remove Nhu. The cable continues: "If, in spite of all your efforts, Diem remains obdurate and refuses, then we must face the possibility that Diem himself cannot be preserved."[17] In fact, beginning in the summer of 1963, Ambassador Lodge and CIA representative Colonel Lucien Conein were in contact with the generals planning a coup against Diem.

At this critical juncture, French President Charles de Gaulle made his first public comment about the Vietnam situation on August 29, 1963. The French statement pointedly referred to France's historic ties with the "country as a whole."[18] United States officials wondered if this reference suggested substantial French support for the Ngos' attempts to establish contact with Hanoi. The American chargé d'affaires in Paris, Cecil Lyon, questioned Claude Lucet, director of political affairs at the French Foreign Ministry (and later ambassador to the United States) on this point. As Lyon reported to Washington: "I now wondered whether

. . . behind scenes France might be conducting covert operation or establishing contact between North and South with view to bringing both sides together." This was "flatly denied" by Lucet who characterized de Gaulle's statement as a "broad definition of long-range policy."[19]

In spite of this denial Lalouette had told Mieczyslaw Maneli, Polish representative to the ICC, that an open dialogue between North and South Vietnam was possible. Maneli conveyed this suggestion to the North Vietnamese in the spring of 1963, and he claims that, by July 1963, some sort of North-South talks had taken place with technical cooperation by the French.[20] Thus, American suspicions of French policy may have been justified.

Nevertheless it is not clear to what extent Lalouette's actions and de Gaulle's August 29 statement were related. As one French commentator wrote at the time: "one can hardly imagine General de Gaulle drafting his historic proclamations under the dictation of an ambassador, however qualified he might be."[21] De Gaulle probably had much less faith in the Ngos than did Lalouette. Foreign Minister Couve de Murville had not been impressed with Ngo Dinh Nhu, whom he met in Paris in 1963. At their meeting, Nhu talked constantly of subjugating his internal enemies; Couve would have preferred to hear about South Vietnam's desire for an independent foreign policy and for improved relations with France.[22] The French foreign minister reportedly remarked after seeing Nhu: "there goes a man with plenty of illusions."[23]

On the other hand, the French were willing to explore all options and hosted in early 1963 a delegation of South Vietnamese parliamentarians who discussed a program of economic and cultural cooperation. According to one commentator, French policy at this time was willing to go "in all directions."[24] De Gaulle met with Lalouette when the latter was in Paris shortly before the August 29 statement was issued and might have been somewhat influenced by him.

The United States continued to express dissatisfaction with Diem's government. President John F. Kennedy publicly voiced his displeasure with Diem in a televised interview with Walter Cronkite on September 3, 1963. Furthermore, Lodge was authorized in September 1963 to take several measures that would pressure Diem into changing his policy. In particular, the United States wanted Diem to end the violent suppression of his internal opponents that culminated in his raid on the Buddhist pagodas in August 1963 and to concentrate on fighting the Viet Cong.

To this end, American officials insisted that Diem send to the field the special forces, trained by United States military personnel and financed by the CIA, which had become Diem's personal palace guard. Without these troops Diem and Nhu were unprotected. Furthermore, the transfer of these troops to the command of the South Vietnamese Joint General Staff in October 1963 placed them under the control of the generals who were plotting Diem's overthrow. Thus, this American action, as well as the partial suspension of American aid to Diem in October 1963, fixed the United States with an element of responsibility for the coup that overthrew him on November 1, 1963.[25]

After Diem's overthrow, French Ambassador Lalouette, who was on leave in France, was summoned to the Foreign Ministry and reprimanded for his over-zealous behavior. Regardless of whether or not they had previously supported Lalouette's machinations, French officials realized that the coup ended any hope of French-South Vietnamese rapprochement. Therefore, Lalouette never returned to Saigon after the November 1 coup.

The overthrow of Diem in November 1963 was a significant factor in de Gaulle's subsequent opposition to American policy in Vietnam. In the first place, it illustrated the bankruptcy of the Saigon regime and its dependence on American support. Second, Diem's successors were required to demonstrate (to the United States as well as their own people) their willingness to prosecute the war with the Vietcong. Consequently, they were openly hostile to suggestions for a negotiated settlement based on neutralization (especially when these suggestions came from France).[26]

It should be emphasized that a policy of rapprochement with the Saigon regime would have been more beneficial to France's considerable interests in South Vietnam than was the hostile posture adopted by de Gaulle after 1963. In 1963, approximately 1,700 French citizens remained in South Vietnam and private French interests dominated the rubber industry, which accounted for 89.6 percent of South Vietnamese exports. France was the second most important country exporting to South Vietnam and operated economic and technical assistance programs as well as giving cultural aid which included the maintenance of *lycées* serving about 30,000 students. Furthermore, those in France with investments in South Vietnam would have preferred that French policy pursue harmonious relations with the regimes that succeeded Diem.

However, the hope that relations between France and South Vietnam might improve died with the Ngo brothers. Diem and Nhu were hardly pro-French; however, they were nationalists who seemed to be resisting United States hegemony in 1963. Warmer relations with France might have been one consequence of this policy. The leaders who replaced the Ngos were totally dependent on the United States; they were free neither in military nor in diplomatic affairs.[27] Hence, by supporting the coup against Diem, the United States had once again reduced the possibilities for French influence in Vietnam.

DE GAULLE'S VIEWS REGARDING THE VIETNAM WAR

De Gaulle's attitude toward Vietnam evolved over time. As head of France's Provisional Government in 1945 and early 1946, he sought to hasten France's return to Indochina. After he retired from politics in January 1946, he continued his support of the Fourth Republic's efforts to retain control of Indochina. However, as the Indochina war progressed, de Gaulle realized that the Viet Minh could not be subdued. In 1953, he met with Jean Sainteny, whose account of events in Vietnam during 1945 and 1946 had just been published. Referring to the book and to Sainteny's earlier conviction that Vietnamese aspirations had to be satisfied, de Gaulle acknowledged: "so it was you who was right."[28]

Furthermore, de Gaulle seemed to extend the lesson France learned in Southeast Asia to other colonial experiences. After he became president of France in 1958, his policy toward French Africa reflected his realization that the forces of national self-determination unleashed by World War II could not be ignored. Within two years after he returned to power he had granted independence to the French colonies south of the Sahara. Although he continued the Algerian war for four more years (1958-62), de Gaulle ended that conflict by granting independence to the Algerian rebels even though the 500,000 French troops there had fought to a standstill. His belief that force was inappropriate to the settlement of political questions was strengthened by the Algerian episode, and he later called upon the United States to follow in Vietnam the example he set by making peace in Algeria.

The key element in de Gaulle's analysis of American involvement in Vietnam during the 1960s was his conviction that the issues at stake there were local. "Our main disagreement with the Americans," said French Foreign Minister Couve de Murville in May 1965, "is on the origin of the conflict. In our opinion, what is happening in South Vietnam is a civil war."[29]

In de Gaulle's view, South Vietnamese President Diem was culpable for rejecting all contact with the North Vietnamese and for permitting the growth of American political influence and military presence in South Vietnam after 1954. Furthermore, none of the governments that followed Diem was able to command internal support or to solve the major external problem, namely, to establish a *modus vivendi* with the regime in the North. Most importantly, the close association of Saigon's leaders with the United States cast doubts on their independence and legitimacy.

Convinced of the essentially political nature of the Vietnamese problem, de Gaulle adamantly opposed all attempts to achieve a military solution. He judged the American military effort futile because, like the Fourth Republic's Indochina war, it avoided the central issue: countering the political appeal of the enemy with a pluralistic political system in South Vietnam. Furthermore, American escalation risked total Indochinese involvement plus possible direct implication of the Soviet Union or China and caused a hardening of positions that dampened the prospects for negotiations.

De Gaulle believed that, contrary to American expectations, harassment of North Vietnam by steady bombing increased the determination of the North Vietnamese. With the atmosphere so poisoned, negotiations became impossible. "Each time there is a new escalation," remarked Foreign Minister Couve de Murville, "negotiations become even more difficult to open."[30]

According to de Gaulle's analysis, a political settlement in Vietnam must be based on the 1954 Geneva principles of non-intervention, reunification, and neutralization. In his view, the large-scale participation of American forces in the Vietnam war was a direct violation of the Geneva principle of non-intervention in Vietnamese affairs. His statements obfuscated the issue of whether American troops had preceded those of North Vietnam in South Vietnam or vice versa, as well as the question of North Vietnam's right to settle South Vietnamese affairs. However, de Gaulle clearly regarded the United States as the foreign invader and advocated an American commitment to withdraw its troops as the precondition for peace talks.

Furthermore, non-intervention implied allowing South Vietnam to form a government more representative than that which existed in Saigon.

France rejected United States claims that the Saigon regime was the legitimate government in South Vietnam. In fact, it blamed the American war effort for obstructing the rights of the South Vietnamese to exercise self-determination.

Distinct from, though related to, the problem of who should govern in South Vietnam, was the question of Vietnamese reunification. De Gaulle believed that a more representative Saigon regime would increase contacts with Hanoi as a prelude to reunification. The French argued (as late as 1968) that North Vietnam would wait as much as ten years after hostilities were concluded for unification to be accomplished. Furthermore, since Hanoi's main goal was reunification, the French believed that North Vietnam might accept a neutralized regime in the South if it could reasonably expect national unity to become a reality.

Finally, de Gaulle urged that a settlement in Vietnam be based on the principle of Indochinese neutralization, which he defined as the removal of Indochina from the sphere of great power conflict. This condition could only work if accompanied by a great power guarantee. Although the French analysis emphasized the local origins of the Vietnam conflict, it did not ignore the wider aspects of the war. In particular, the French realized that China, the Soviet Union, and the United States each had distinct interests in Indochina, which had to be recognized in any settlement.

French statements concerning an Indochina settlement spoke of including the "five world powers" (the United States, the Soviet Union, China, France, and Britain) who would have to cooperate in its execution and in the postwar development of the area. The credentials that entitled France to membership in the club of the "five" were historical ties in the area, global concerns, and, especially, contacts with all the necessary parties.[31]

The French emphasized the importance of Chinese participation in any Indochinese settlement and the necessity of a minimal Sino-American understanding concerning Southeast Asia. Convinced that Peking must be reintegrated into the international community, France renewed its own diplomatic relations with China in January 1964 and urged the United States to do likewise. Subsequently, the French became convinced that in Chinese eyes, peace in Vietnam required a unilateral American action that would indicate the United States ultimate intention to withdraw from the area. This view rested on the assumption that the Chinese were

not pursuing expansionist aims in Asia, a judgment directly contrary to
that of American leaders until 1969.

De Gaulle reasoned that after an understanding was reached among the
interested powers based on the principles of non-intervention, neutrality,
and reunification, an agreement could be drawn up which would include
provisions for its implementation. Presumably, procedures would be
established for reporting violations of the accord and for summoning
the signatory nations to exert their collective influence against the viola-
tor. However, his proposals were based on the assumption that if the
accords corresponded to the claims of the interested powers, particularly
the Asian states, it would be in everyone's interest to uphold them. Furthermore, stability could be encouraged in Indochina by means of a long-
term cooperative effort to develop the area's future and would focus
attention on the most grievous problems facing governments there. This
entailed Western participation with at least tacit Chinese consent, and it
would be another step in improving relations with China and encouraging
its reintegration into the international community.

In sum, de Gaulle's prescriptions for peace in Vietnam depended on
the fulfillment of certain conditions by the United States. These he formulated in his speech at Phnompenh on September 1, 1966, and in his
press conference of October 28, 1966. They included

1. acceptance of the principle of Vietnamese self-determination
2. withdrawal of American troops
3. acceptance of controlled neutrality for Southeast Asia
4. recognition of the necessity of dealing with China.

These conditions indicate the disparity between de Gaulle's analysis
and that of the United States (prior to the Nixon administration). His
attitude toward the requirements of self-determination implied his doubts
about the legitimacy of the South Vietnamese government to which
American support was pledged. His appeal for an American commitment
to withdraw as a prior condition for settlement accused the United States
of "foreign intervention" and acquitted the North Vietnamese of that
charge while the American effort in Vietnam purported to be a response
to North Vietnamese aggression. His desire for controlled neutrality in
Southeast Asia was contrary to American support for a non-Communist
regime in Saigon. Finally, his suggestion of an approach to China assumed
the defensive character of Chinese responses in Southeast Asia whereas
American policy in the 1960s was portrayed as a response to the threat

of Chinese imperialism. The distance which separated France's prescriptions for the Vietnamese situation from those of the United States resulted from their distinctly opposite interpretations of events in Indochina.

SUPPORT WITHIN FRANCE FOR DE GAULLE'S VIEWS ON VIETNAM

General de Gaulle's attitudes toward the conflict in Vietnam reflected those of most Frenchmen. In France, public distaste for the war was inspired by concern for the human suffering it caused among people for whom the French felt some affection; consequently, French public opinion objected most violently to American bombing of North Vietnam. Furthermore, the French knew from their own government's experiences in Indochina and Algeria that wars against determined local dissidents are not easily won. Finally, there was some sympathy in France for the plight of a small, primitive people resisting the American colossus. Thus, like de Gaulle, the French disapproved of United States policy in Vietnam.

THE PRESS

During the 1960s, the Parisian press was almost unanimous in its criticism of the American role in Vietnam. There was general agreement with de Gaulle's analysis of the Vietnam situation and his recommendations for a settlement.

Most French journalists regarded the conflict as a civil war that could not be settled militarily, and they did not believe that the bombing policy was the correct tactic to achieve negotiations. Some of them had spent years observing Vietnamese affairs and they were critical of the Saigon regime's refusal to recognize internal resistance as its real enemy and to seek an accommodation with the National Liberation Front (NLF). Although the Gaullist *La Nation* and the Communist *l'Humanité* were most strongly in agreement with de Gaulle regarding the civil nature of the conflict, this opinion was shared by the more moderate papers, such as *Le Monde* and *Combat.* In addition, more conservative papers, such as *La Croix* and the normally pro-American *Le Figaro,* exhibited a distaste for the war which was based on the belief that an American victory could not exterminate opposition to the Saigon regime.

The French press became especially hostile to American policy in Viet-

nam in early 1965 when regular bombing of North Vietnam began and
American ground participation in the war increased. In accord with their
view that the problem in Vietnam was political, most French journalists
doubted that military escalation could succeed. Thus, as *Le Monde* edi-
torialized on April 3, 1965,

To respond to the action of terrorists and guerillas by a series of massive
air attacks on the other side of the border, is to wage a very different kind
of war from that which strikes at the imminent adversary in order to
rapidly hit him.[32]

Moreover, *Le Monde* continued, this tactic was logical only if it was considered as one step in a further escalation that might have as its climax the
bombing of Chinese territory. Thus, like de Gaulle, *Le Monde* speculated
that United States strategy included a steadily widened war.

Doubts about the efficacy of escalation and fears of its consequences
led French journalists to suspect that the United States did not sincerely
advocate unconditional negotiations. The timing of peace moves was often
suspect in French eyes. Even *Le Figaro* sometimes wondered about the
credibility of peace moves.[33] French journalists seemed to share de
Gaulle's view that the United States was losing the war psychologically
because escalation was inconsistent with negotiation. They reasoned that
the bombing was an ineffective instrument if the object was negotiation.

The similarity between France's Indochina war and the one in which
the United States became involved was apparent to the French journalists
who had covered the earlier war. They believed that the United States
must heed the lesson France learned in Algeria and Indochina, viz., that
it is necessary to negotiate with those you are fighting, regardless of your
opinion of them.[34] The adamant refusal of the United States to meet with
the NLF was regarded as further proof of the insincerity of American
efforts to begin negotiations.

Although French newspapers agreed with de Gaulle's analysis of the
Vietnam war, they did not wholeheartedly support his public posture
vis à vis the United States role there. In particular, some journalists objected to his strident criticism of United States policy; such objections
usually appeared in journals that were moderately anti-Gaullist. For example, *Le Figaro*'s distaste for the conflict did not obscure its criticism
of de Gaulle's bitter anti-Americanism and of his "bitter picture of Amer-

ica's role in Southeast Asia."[35] *Le Figaro* argued that de Gaulle had not made clear his advocacy of withdrawal by all three big powers involved in Vietnam—China, Russia, and the United States—but had made it appear as if he referred only to the last.

Though editorially more complacent than *Le Figaro* about the logic of de Gaulle's Vietnam statements, *Le Monde* was not always enthusiastic about their tone. Furthermore, *Le Monde* voiced doubts about de Gaulle's effectiveness, reminding its readers of the unpredictability of events beyond his control. Thus, *Le Monde* shared a view held by many Frenchmen that the United States would not succeed any better than France had in imposing a military solution on Vietnam but cautioned against cherishing too many illusions concerning the conditions for a political solution. Although *Le Monde* editorially supported de Gaulle's proposal for neutralization of all Southeast Asia, it questioned whether France possessed any means that might obtain a settlement.[36]

POLITICAL AND PUBLIC OPINION

The political Right in France was somewhat divided over the Vietnam issue. The classic or extreme Right, including both strong nationalists and extremely pro-American elements favored the war and was careful to avoid criticizing American policy. The Gaullists, following the government's example, criticized both the course of the war and the goals and methods of United States policy there. Those who found themselves between the classic Right and the Gaullists, such as M. Valéry Giscard d'Estaing, wrestled with their position in silence and equivocated in public.[37]

In some pro-American but anti-Gaullist circles, criticism of American involvement in Southeast Asia focused on the fear that the United States would neglect its European obligations. These anti-Gaullists accused de Gaulle of desiring this outcome which would leave France a freer hand in Europe. Furthermore, Jean Lecanuet, whose 1965 presidential campaign emphasized Atlanticist and "European" themes, was more directly critical of de Gaulle. He termed the General's statements, "irritating, fruitless, and inopportune anti-Americanism,"[38] and he criticized de Gaulle's willingness to accept Communization of Vietnam as the price for peace. Relating Vietnam to the issue of European unity, Lecanuet argued that France's Vietnam policy should be coordinated with that of other European countries.

The French Left, though unanimously opposed to the conflict in Vietnam, did not agree regarding the manner in which to oppose United States policy. The extreme Left—Parti Communiste Français (PCF), L'Union Nationale des Etudiants de la France (UNEF), and Parti Socialiste Unifié (PSU)—upheld the positions of South Vietnam's National Liberation Front which placed them in diametric opposition to American policy. The more moderate Left—Federation de la Gauche Democratique et Socialiste (FGDS), Section Française de l'Internationale Ouvrière (SFIO), and Radicaux—avoided extreme anti-Americanism. These various Leftist opinions clashed at a colloquium organized in 1966 to protest the war, and the more moderate elements succeeded in arranging a compromise declaration that did not sound as harsh as some would have wished. The line of distinction among these Leftist groups was not the traditional boundary between Communist and Socialist, but rather between those who followed Moscow's line and those who chose Peking's. In particular, the French Communist party risked losing control of the extreme opposition to the war "if not to the Left, to the East."[39]

In later years, there was increased unity among traditional Leftist groups; after 1971, the Parti Socialiste (the new name of the SFIO after 1969) joined with the PCF and more extreme organizations in forums which protested the war. Leftist disunity regarding the Vietnam issue was a function of the internecine warfare that typically besets French politics of the Left. Moreover, Vietnam posed a dilemma for de Gaulle's Leftist critics since their differences with him were stylistic rather than substantial. Thus, Vietnam was essentially preempted from the political arena in France because de Gaulle's views had so much support; even the Communists found themselves substantially in agreement with him.[40]

Opinion polls in France after 1966 showed mounting public concern about the Vietnam situation and opposition to the course of United States policy in Southeast Asia. In September 1966, 68 percent of those questioned said the United States should begin to withdraw its troops from Vietnam; one year later the percentage had risen to 72 percent.[41] In 1967, France ranked fourth among those countries whose citizens sought a United States withdrawal from Vietnam (after Finland, Sweden, and Brazil).

From 1966 to the start of the peace talks in 1968, periodic mass demonstrations protesting the war were held near the American embassy in Paris. These were sometimes violent and reached their peak during Vice-

President Humphrey's visit to Paris in April 1967. Subsequently, the Paris
police limited the bounds of demonstrations, outlawing them entirely
after the peace talks began. These public gatherings were often Communist-
organized but they garnered support from various quarters of French
opinion. In addition, opposition to American actions in Vietnam was expressed by hundreds of petitions bearing thousands of signatures which
were delivered to the American embassy by mail or in person each week.[42]

As was the case when opposition to the Algerian war was mounted in
France, numerous ad hoc organizations were formed to oppose the war in
Vietnam. These included "Le Comité Vietnam National," led by Jean-
Paul Sartre, which was in the vanguard of public opposition to the Vietnam war; "Le Millard pour le Vietnam," formed in October 1966 by a
group of engineers and researchers with the aim of raising a million francs
to aid the Vietnamese; "Le Comité français pour le soutien du peuple
vietnamien" which, together with "le Mouvement contre l'armement
atomique," organized a boycott of United States products; and "le Mouvement de la paix," closely related to the Communist party, which was
responsible for many of the mass demonstrations and for hundreds of
petitions urging that the United States put an end to the bombing and
withdraw from Vietnam.

The currents of French opposition to American policy in Vietnam
reached different levels and encompassed a wide range of sentiments.
According to Jean Lacouture the elements of this critical opinion may
be classified into the following four categories: first, concern over the
horrors suffered by all Vietnamese as a result of the wartime situation;
second, sympathy for the Vietnamese forces facing tremendous American
superiority; third, suspicion of the motives behind American escalations;
and, fourth, anti-Americanism on the part of the extremes of Right and
Left, e.g., the ultra-nationalists and the Communists.[43] Most important
was the Frenchmen's pity for the suffering of the poor Vietnamese people, so long beleaguered by foreigners. Also, the French experienced a
sense of futility regarding American policy in Vietnam that must have
recalled the later years of France's own struggle there. The policy of
bombing North Vietnam brought together these sentiments; the hardship
imposed upon a helpless people seemed futile as well as cruel. Thus, opposition to America's Vietnam policy crystallized over the American bombing
policy. This climate of opinion in France was sympathetic to de Gaulle's
public criticism of the United States role in Vietnam.

Added to the historic legacy of discord between France and the United States concerning Indochina from World War II until the French withdrawal from Vietnam in 1956 was their continued disagreement in the early years of the Fifth Republic. In the 1958-63 period, the two countries disagreed regarding the resolution of the 1960-62 Laotian crises and their policy was at odds in 1963 when American support for the coup against President Diem ended the possibility of resurgent French influence in Saigon. Furthermore, the November 1, 1963, coup and its aftermath of political instability in South Vietnam increased de Gaulle's pessimism regarding the ability of the Saigon regime to broaden its political base and subdue its enemies on the battlefield.

In fact, de Gaulle's analysis of the Vietnam situation, evolved over time and influenced by France's own experiences in Indochina and Algeria, contrasted sharply with American assumptions about the political and military situation in Southeast Asia. These distinct French and American perspectives had been evident since 1940. The gap between the two countries on this issue widened as the United States became more directly involved in military support of an anti-Communist regime in Saigon. Significantly, de Gaulle's criticism of this American policy, particularly its reliance on foreign military means to solve indigenous political problems was supported by political and public opinion in France.

NOTES

1. Roger Hilsman, *To Move a Nation* (New York: Doubleday, 1967), pp. 105-126, and Arthur J. Dommen, *Conflict in Laos: The Politics of Neutralization* (New York: Praeger, 1964), pp. 276-278. Hilsman's account of these and subsequent events in Laos is especially interesting in view of his role in formulating United States policy toward Laos during his tenure as chief of the Intelligence and Research Bureau of the State Department, 1961-63, and as assistant secretary of state for Far Eastern affairs, 1963-64.

2. Bernard Fall, *Anatomy of a Crisis: The Laotian Crisis of 1960-61* (New York: Doubleday, 1969), p. 147. In this work, Fall describes vividly French-American differences regarding Laos.

3. Ibid., p. 214.

4. One manifestation of French-American differences over Laos is the treatment each country gave Prince Souvanna Phouma who made a world tour in the spring of 1961. Paris accorded him an official high level welcome and de Gaulle met personally with him for a long conference. Washington's plans for his visit were much more casual and provided that he be met at the airport only by a low-level State Department employee, contrary to the practice at his other stops (which included

Moscow and New Delhi). Bernard Fall concludes that it was this American attitude which caused the prince to cancel his visit to the United States (*Anatomy of a Crisis*, pp. 221-224). Thus, on the eve of the Geneva talks, the French were firm in their support of the neutralist Souvanna Phouma while the Americans, still unsure of his credentials, withheld judgment.

5. At the suggestion of Cambodia's Prince Sihanouk in January 1961, the membership of the 1954 Geneva conference was expanded to include the members of the ICC (Canada, Poland, and India) and those of Laos' neighbors which had not participated in the earlier meeting (Burma and Thailand). Thus the fourteen powers who considered the Laotian question at Geneva in 1961-62 were the United States, United Kingdom, France, Canada, Republic of (South) Vietnam, Democratic Republic of (North) Vietnam, Thailand, Soviet Union, China, Poland, Burma, India, Cambodia, and Laos.

6. Fall, *Anatomy of a Crisis*, p. 216.

7. George Modelski, *International Conference on the Settlement of the Laotian Question, 1961-62*, (Canberra: Australian National University, 1962), p. 20. Modelski states that the United States avoided the first few sessions of this group "seemingly to avoid associating with China, or else not to be drawn prematurely into discussions on the Declaration of Neutrality." (Ibid.) He is very critical of United States policy during the conference on the grounds that America sacrificed its functions of leadership because of lack of resolve.

8. For a discussion of the French role at the Vietnam peace negotiations see Chapter 5.

9. Interview with Ellen Hammer, Paris, July 4, 1972.

10. Interview with Roger Lalouette, Versailles, July 19, 1972.

11. Ibid.

12. *United States-Vietnam Relations 1945-1967: Study Prepared by the Department of Defense* (Washington, D.C.: U.S. Government Printing Office, 1971), Book IV, B.5, p. 2.

13. Central Intelligence Agency Information Report No. TDCSDB 3/654,285 April 22, 1963. National Security Council Country Files, Vietnam, Box 198, John F. Kennedy Library.

14. Interview with Ambassador Roger Lalouette. Ho made this remark in a conversation with Ram Chundur Goburdhun, the Indian representative on the ICC. Mr. Goburdhun relayed his conversation with Ho to Ambassador Lalouette.

15. Georges Chaffard notes that the American press, especially columnist Joseph Alsop, blamed Lalouette for stirring up trouble in Saigon. Georges Chaffard, *Les deux guerres du Vietnam: de Valluy à Westmoreland* (Paris: La Table Ronde, 1969), pp. 317-320.

16. *United States-Vietnam Relations 1945-1967*, Book IV, B.5, p. 15.

17. Ibid.

18. *Chronology of the Major French Statements on Vietnam Since August, 1963* (New York: French Embassy, 1968), p. 5.

19. Department of State telegram No. 1037, September 4, 1963, Box 199 (vols. XV-XVI). National Security Council Country Files, Vietnam, John F. Kennedy Library.

20. Mieczyslaw Maneli, *War of the Vanquished* (New York: Harper and Row, 1971), pp. 121-127.

21. Henri Marque writing in *Paris-Presse*, September 6, 1963.

22. Interview with Etienne Manac'h, Paris, July 27, 1972. In 1963, Ambassador Manac'h was director of the Asian Division of the French Foreign Ministry. It was he who arranged the meeting between Couve and Nhu.

23. Chaffard, *Les deux guerres*, p. 303.

24. Ibid., p. 305. Chaffard later mentions a secret meeting between de Gaulle and the South Vietnamese ambassador to France in late October 1963 in which the French president asked what immediate assistance France could give to the Saigon regime. P. 336.

25. *United States-Vietnam Relations 1945-1967*, Book IV, B. 5, p. 35.

26. Criticism of French policy by South Vietnamese leaders immediately follow- ing the coup can be explained in terms of their need to reject solutions based on neutralization so as to demonstrate their anti-Communism to the United States. See the articles by Jean Lacouture in *Le Monde*, January 16, 1964, and by Max Clos in *Le Figaro*, December 21, 1963.

27. See George McT. Kahin, "The Pentagon Papers: A Critical Evaluation," *American Political Science Review* 69, no. 2 (June 1975), p. 682-684.

28. Quoted in Jean Lacouture, *De Gaulle* (New York: Avon Books, 1968), p. 215, and confirmed by Jean Sainteny in an interview in Paris, June 26, 1972.

29. "Statement . . . before the NATO Council, May 12, 1965," French Embassy, Press and Information Division, *Chronology*, p. 9.

30. "Interview . . . (Europe No. 1), September 19, 1966," *Chronology*, p. 22.

31. De Gaulle mentioned these qualifications in his press conference on Sep- tember 9, 1965.

32. *Le Monde*, April 3, 1965, p. 1.

33. For example, see the column by *Le Figaro's* Washington correspondent, Nicholas Chatelain, February 1, 1966, p. 5, and by Roger Massip, February 2, 1966, p. 4.

34. *Le Monde*, April 9, 1965, p. 1. Although French journalists recognized the parallels between their country's involvement in Indochina and that of the United States, they were also aware of the dissimilarities. Few argued, as did *l'Humanité*, that the Americans would be defeated as the French were at Dien Bien Phu. Instead, the majority of French reporting on Vietnam in the 1960s pictured an endless war of attrition which neither side could win.

35. July 24, 1966, p. 5.

36. Editorial by SIRIUS (former editor-in-chief Hubert Beuve-Méry), February 2-3, 1964, p. 1.

37. Giscard's attempts to split hairs in order to emphasize the differences be- tween his Independent Republicans and the Gaullists earned him the title, *M. de Oui-Mais* (Mr. Yes-But), given him by the satirical weekly, *Le Canard Enchainé*.

38. *Le Monde*, September 11-12, 1966.

39. Jean Lacouture, "L'Opinion Française et la seconde guerre du Vietnam," *Le Monde*, December 13, 1966, p. 3. These new divisions among the French Leftists were again manifested eighteen months after Lacouture wrote when extreme Maoist

elements incited the student-worker disturbances of May 1968 over the opposition of more moderate leaders, including the Moscow-oriented PCF.

40. For example, at their Eighteenth Annual Congress in January 1967, the PCF praised de Gaulle "without reservation" for his Vietnam policy. *New York Times,* January 9, 1967, p. 16.

41. *Sondages: revue française de l'opinion publique,* 1967, p. 68.

42. During the summer of 1967, the author (an intern in the Political Section of the American embassy in Paris) was responsible for receiving and examining these petitions and can attest to their vehemence.

43. Lacouture, "L'Opinion Francais . . . ," p. 1.

PART III | SITUATIONAL FACTORS

Chapter 4

Escalation and Major American Ground Involvement

DE GAULLE'S REACTION TO AMERICAN ESCALATION IN VIETNAM, 1965-68

THE FRENCH CRITIQUE OF AMERICAN POLICY

Given de Gaulle's views on Vietnam described in the previous chapter and his attitude toward the United States discussed in Chapter 1, it is not surprising that he adopted a stance strongly critical of United States policy in Vietnam during the 1960s. The situation in Vietnam during the period of American escalation provided an illustration of the American will to hegemony and an opportunity for France to dissociate itself from an American policy with which it disagreed. De Gaulle's critique of United States policy was not pejorative—it was based on sincere conviction and supported by French opinion. However, it also served his wider aim of opposing American hegemony in all quarters.

Substantively, Vietnam provided an example of the United States tendency to which de Gaulle objected in NATO—that of equating allied interests with its own. The United States assumed that its European and SEATO allies would support its policy in Vietnam and justified its actions there on the basis of defending the common burden. However, as de Gaulle made clear, the United States could not take French support for granted on Asian matters any more than on those relating to Europe. On the contrary, de Gaulle sought to prevent French involvement in a wider war which might result from military escalation by the United States in Vietnam. It was partially to avoid involvement in a conflict not of his choosing that de Gaulle withdrew from NATO in 1966.

Stylistically, Vietnam was an ideal opportunity for France to express foreign policy views distinct from those of the United States. American actions in Vietnam were controversial and inspired criticism in many quarters. De Gaulle's public statements regarding Vietnam became harsher in response to deepening American military involvement. In some cases his public criticism had been preceded by private warnings to American officials which went unheeded; thus, he could argue that his criticism was warranted. The object of his critique was not to influence a change in American tactics which would lead to peace talks; this he believed would come about only if the United States perceived its interests differently. Rather, for de Gaulle, in Vietnam as elsewhere, his critical posture was his policy.

De Gaulle reserved his sharpest public criticism of United States policy in Vietnam until after American escalation in 1965. Prior to that, his statements reproached the United States only indirectly. He presented his views to American officials in private.[1] Certainly, the latter were aware of his opinions regarding Indochina, especially after the Laotian crisis. Also, according to de Gaulle, he warned President Kennedy when the two met in Paris on May 31, 1961, not to become deeply involved in Vietnam. In his words:

For you, I told him, intervention in this region will be an entanglement without end. From the moment that nations have awakened, no foreign authority, whatever its means, has any chance of imposing itself on them. You are going to see this.[2]

Over two years later, on August 29, 1963, de Gaulle first commented publicly on the situation in South Vietnam. As mentioned, his remarks were ill-timed from the American perspective and implied French support for rapprochement between North and South, which was contrary to American policy. However, the only reference to the United States was a phrase suggesting that Vietnam's problems should be settled "independently of the outside."[3] There was no direct criticism of American policy in the August 29 statement.

Throughout 1964, de Gaulle warned the United States privately and in public about the dangers of escalation. In a meeting in Paris with American Undersecretary of State George Ball in June 1964, de Gaulle cautioned that military escalation would involve the United States in a direct conflict with North Vietnam and prolong the war; he made this warning public in a press conference on July 23, less than three weeks before the Gulf of Tonkin incidents. The American response to these events, together with subsequent American escalation, in particular the dispatch of American ground troops to South Vietnam and the beginning of regular bombing raids against North Vietnam in early 1965, confirmed de Gaulle's suspicion that the United States sought military victory at the expense of a negotiated settlement. Thereafter, de Gaulle became sharply critical of United States policy in Vietnam.[4]

De Gaulle urged publicly and privately that President Johnson explore opportunities for peace talks. One such opportunity was a thirty-seven day bombing pause in December 1965 and January 1966 during which Johnson sent ambassadors Arthur Goldberg and Averell Harriman to explore the possibilities for negotiations with various heads of state. One of Goldberg's stops was Paris, and he carried a letter from President Johnson to General de Gaulle. Before it could be delivered, de Gaulle presented Goldberg with a secret letter to Johnson urging that the United States prolong the bombing halt indefinitely to encourage Hanoi to open talks.

De Gaulle delayed answering the note Goldberg brought to him from Johnson until his own letter had been dealt with. The American response came on January 31, 1966, in the form of a resumption of the bombing raids. Angered, de Gaulle sent Johnson a note highly critical of United States policy whose tone *Le Monde* described as "blistering."[5] Undoubtedly, de Gaulle had waited almost a month to write in the hope that his suggestion for an indefinite bombing pause might be acted upon; the harsh tone of his letter reflected his disappointment that, once again, the United States chose military escalation instead of negotiations.

About seven months later, in his Phnompenh speech, de Gaulle called publicly for an American initiative that could lead to peace talks—unilateral American withdrawal from Vietnam. In his words, the opening of peace talks depended on "the decision and the commitment which American would have wanted to take beforehand to repatriate its forces within a suitable and determined period of time."[6]

Delivered to an audience of 100,000 in Phnompenh stadium during

de Gaulle's stop there on a world tour, the speech was written by de
Gaulle himself and contained his most comprehensive critique of American policy in Vietnam. Emphasizing the internal nature of the struggle,
he underscored his disagreement with the American charge that the war
involved outside aggression. The events of the previous summer, when
American troop levels reached 300,000 and the United States bombed
oil storage depots at Hanoi and Haiphong, must have been in de Gaulle's
mind when he said:

Illusions about the use of force led to the continual reinforcement of the
expeditionary corps and to increasingly extensive escalation in Asia, increasingly closer to China, increasingly provoking in the eyes of the Soviet
Union, increasingly censured by numerous peoples of Europe, Africa,
and Latin America and, in the final analysis, increasingly menacing for the
peace of the world.[7]

These words reflect de Gaulle's uneasiness about the misuse of American
power and his apprehension lest France, as an American ally, become involved in a widened conflict. At Phnompenh he specifically cited France's
"determination not to be wherever it may be and whatever may happen,
automatically implicated in the eventual extension of the drama and,
in any event, to keep her hands free."[8]

Furthermore, in his Phnompenh speech, de Gaulle called attention
to the example set by France in Algeria "by deliberately putting an end
to sterile fighting on a ground that, nonetheless, her forces unquestionably
dominated, that she had directly administered for one hundred and thirty-
two years and where more than a million of her children were settled."[9]
The French in Algeria, no less than the Americans in Vietnam, were not
on the verge of defeat; rather, they realized that the fighting there would
have no positive result, and they thereby ended it simply by deciding to
leave. De Gaulle suggested that the Americans do likewise in Vietnam.

There were certain similarities between the two situations. The Fourth
Republic poured thousands of men into Algeria and repeatedly promised
a victory which seemed illusory in a scenario that resembled the United
States effort in Southeast Asia. France's leaders, including de Gaulle, refused to recognize the Algerian rebels as the United States rejected negotiations with the Viet Cong; American policy moved toward acceptance
of the negotiations with the NLF as the French had finally agreed to meet

with the Algerians. Finally, the bombing of North Vietnam, which betrayed Washington's failure to distinguish between North Vietnamese and local dissidents, may be compared to the 1956 Suez expedition which indicated France's exaggeration of the importance of Nasser's aid to the Algerian rebels.[10]

The Algerian example was ideal from de Gaulle's point of view; it illustrated his credentials as a commentator on the Vietnam war, and it provided an example of the unilateral initiative he proposed for the United States in Southeast Asia. Negotiations had become possible in Algeria once the French realized that they could not win the war; de Gaulle believed that the United States must come to a similar realization regarding Vietnam before peace talks would be possible.[11]

After his Phnompenh speech in September 1966, de Gaulle and his spokesman added no new elements to France's public posture regarding Vietnam. His statements on the subject in 1967 were less lengthy and not as dramatic as previously with one exception: after the Arab-Israeli war in June 1967, de Gaulle linked the war with the conflict in Vietnam. Charging the United States with responsibility for both wars, de Gaulle said on June 21, 1967:

The war unleashed in Vietnam by American intervention, the destruction of lives and property that it entails, the fundamental sterility that stamps it, however powerful may be the means employed and however terrible may be their effects, cannot fail to spread the trouble, not only locally but at a distance.

Hence, the attitude of China and the haste of its armaments. Hence, on the other hand, the psychological and political process that resulted in the struggle in the Middle East.[12]

These remarks reflected de Gaulle's displeasure that the Vietnam war impeded developments favorable to his own foreign policy initiatives, in particular, an atmosphere of détente and international fluidity in which he might challenge the United States and also pursue rapprochement with the Soviet Union or China.[13]

There were advantages for France in adopting a position similar to that of the Soviets regarding the 1967 Mideast war. The rapport between the two countries on this issue as on Vietnam was manifest when Premier Kosygin conferred with General de Gaulle in Paris enroute to and from

the United Nations General Assembly's special session in June 1967.
Kosygin declared that his talks with the French president showed a community of positions, especially regarding Vietnam on which he discerned,
"a definite coincidence in the positions of our countries."[14]

Nevertheless, de Gaulle's policy depended on the correct mix of Soviet-
American cooperation and conflict; too much of either restricted French
action. Furthermore, he viewed global politics in the mid and late 1960s
as dominated by American power which he believed to be misapplied in
Vietnam. Therefore, he adopted a posture strongly critical of American
conduct of the war.

THE AMERICAN REACTION

American officials believed that de Gaulle's Vietnam policy was one
more attempt to embarrass the United States. His bitter rhetoric concerning Vietnam was reminiscent of his opposition to American policy
in NATO and Europe, and many American officials did not listen to the
message it contained. De Gaulle's pronouncements on Vietnam had a
doctrinaire quality that American officials found most disquieting; their
numerous consultations with the French left them with the impression
that the Gaullist mind was closed on the Vietnam issue.[15] Furthermore,
United States officials did not believe that French advice on Vietnam was
disinterested. They reasoned that the French were ashamed of their own
defeat in Indochina and, consequently, did not wish to see the United
States achieve the victory that eluded France. French expertise regarding
Indochina was dismissed by American officials as outdated, and de
Gaulle's pessimistic estimates regarding American success in the war
were rejected as vindictive.

In fact, France's own experiences in Indochina probably did influence
de Gaulle's estimate of the American role there in the 1960s. He was
aware of the difficulties of opposing the forces of national resistance because of the French-Viet Minh struggle and due to the Algerian war. Furthermore, the repeated divergence of French-American interests in Indochina after 1940 led de Gaulle to conclude that the United States sought
to supplant French influence in Indochina. He accused the Americans of
"an aversion to any colonial work which had not been theirs," and asserted
that "the natural desire in such a powerful people to ensure themselves
of new positions determined the Americans to take our place in Indo-

china."[16] Considering this view, the American expectation during the 1960s that France should support the United States in a conflict against Ho Chi Minh must have seemed ludicrous to General de Gaulle.

American mistrust of French intentions is illustrated by Undersecretary of State George Ball's reaction to his June 1964 meeting with de Gaulle. Ball had told the French president that the United States had but two choices in Vietnam: either shore up the Saigon government politically and militarily or commit the full weight of United States power to the South Vietnamese effort. De Gaulle, in turn, had warned against any military escalation which he regarded as futile and he told Ball that there was a third alternative, namely, to avoid direct American involvement by accepting the French suggestion that the Geneva conference be reconvened.[17]

Although Ball himself preferred negotiation to escalation, he evidently chafed at the French president's suggestion. On October 5, 1964, four months after his visit to Paris, he drafted a State Department memorandum urging that multilateral negotiations be arranged specifically without the participation of the French government. He wrote:

I do not suggest that we approach the French government. Certainly de Gaulle's policy will be to try to bring about maximum, rather than minimum, cost to United States prestige. It is important that we design our plan of action in such a manner as to avoid having it appear as a French diplomatic victory.[18]

This hostile estimate of French intentions regarding Vietnam undoubtedly carried over from French-American disagreements in other quarters. Undersecretary Ball, a well-known advocate of European unity, had once served as counsel to the European communities; his belief that de Gaulle sought to damage United States prestige undoubtedly reflected his impatience with France's European policy.[19]

Furthermore, United States officials saw French comments on Vietnam as part of de Gaulle's grand scheme to reduce the international influence of the United States. In a speech on March 17, 1965, Ball characterized de Gaulle's Vietnam statements as irresponsible criticism from a nation which sought to restore its prewar influence at the expense of the United States by weakening or dismantling the institutions through which Europe and America cooperate.[20] He argued that American commitments abroad could be reduced if a united Europe resumed its worldwide responsibilities. This line of reasoning falsely assumed that a European federation would always be a willing supporter of American policies beyond Europe. In fact, it was precisely this American tendency—to equate allied interests with those of the United States and to subjugate Europe to America's global policy aims—that de Gaulle had always resisted.

De Gaulle's Phnompenh speech reinforced the American belief that French policy on Vietnam was one-sided. President Johnson quickly responded to the demand for a unilateral American departure by saying that he would announce his timetable for withdrawal when the Communists offered theirs.[21] He had cause to view the Phnompenh speech with hostility: shortly before de Gaulle left for Asia, Secretary Rusk had written to French Foreign Minister Couve de Murville suggesting American willingness to arrange for mutual troop withdrawals. The Rusk letter mentioned two possible formulas by which an American withdrawal might be arranged: first, in accord with a negotiated mutual "withdrawal by phases" to be verified by an international authority, or second, by a secretly arranged, phased "unilateral" withdrawal which both sides would observe.[22] De Gaulle's remarks in Phnompenh ignored this letter; clearly he had no desire to be "Washington's spokesman," while he was in Cambodia.[23]

Furthermore, de Gaulle did not believe that the Rusk letter went far enough. In particular, there had been no modification of American policy on the crucial matter of the Viet Cong's role in the conflict. The French considered the distinction between North Vietnamese and NLF forces central to the issue of troop withdrawals. In their view the South Vietnamese government was primarily fighting the National Liberation Front; the war originated because "the South Vietnamese people revolted against their government."[24] Thus, some recognition by the United States of the political nature of South Vietnam's problems and of the diverse interests of the parties involved would have been necessary before de Gaulle would transmit an American offer to the other side. As Couve de Murville said, "In order for us to say something to the Vietnamese it would be necessary for us to believe it."[25] Clearly, with regard to the United States intent to withdraw from Indochina, the French in 1966, according to Couve de Murville, "knew it wasn't true."[26]

In spite of France's public opposition to American policy, President Johnson, in his remarks about the Phnompenh speech, avoided any references to the Rusk letter. Instead, he suggested the possibility of scheduled *mutual* withdrawals, thus telling the North Vietnamese in public what he had hoped de Gaulle would tell them in private.[27] Since it was only after the Phnompenh speech that Johnson distinctly spoke of a scheduled withdrawal, de Gaulle's refusal may have edged Johnson into a public posture he might otherwise have avoided.

After the Phnompenh speech, de Gaulle added no new elements to his harsh critique of American policy in Vietnam. French-American relations had deteriorated on all fronts—de Gaulle had announced France's intention to withdraw from NATO in March 1966—and they did not improve until after President Johnson announced a pause in the bombing of Vietnam in March 1968. An indication of the deep distrust between French and Americans between 1966 and 1968 were the events that marred Vice-President Humphrey's visit to Paris in April 1967. Although his official welcome and talks with de Gaulle were ostensibly friendly, the vice-president encountered numerous street demonstrations protesting America's Vietnam policy. Humphrey met demonstrators at almost every stop he made in Paris; on one occasion, eggs, paint, and stones were hurled at his car, and on another, an American flag taken from the American Cathedral was burned. Two American Marines, who formed an honor guard when Humphrey placed a wreath before a statue of George Washington, were attacked by the demonstrators; the American embassy officially protested to the Paris police who reportedly stood by without aiding the victims. The police later responded with an apology. Although Humphrey had met demonstrators everywhere in Europe, those in Paris were the most violent, and they probably dissipated what goodwill the visit had generated.

Furthermore the flag-burning incident prompted a response from an irate American citizen who burned a French flag outside the French consulate in Chicago. Although public American sentiment toward de Gaulle is beyond the scope of this study, expression was not confined to isolated acts by individuals: for example, in September 1967 the American Legion urged diplomatic and economic retaliation against French policy, and in December 1967 in a speech on the floor of the House of Representatives, Congressman Mendel Rivers urged that the bodies of American war dead buried in France be disinterred and returned to the United States! The American fashion industry periodically raised the question of an organized boycott of French clothes, and American tourism in France fell as many travelers chose to avoid Paris. All these instances indicate that the average American citizen, usually unconcerned with foreign policy, reacted strongly to what was perceived as the insulting behavior of General de Gaulle toward the United States.

In spite of these popular feelings and of the sharpness with which French and American views on Vietnam diverged, officials on both sides of the Atlantic minimized the depth of their disagreement. President Johnson was determined "not to fuss with the General if I can help it,"[28] and he maintained this resolve throughout his presidency. In his memoirs, President Johnson wrote:

I made it a rule for myself and for the U.S. Government simply to ignore President de Gaulle's attack on our policies and the doubts he had raised about the value of our pledges.[29]

De Gaulle and his spokesmen frequently mentioned that they spoke of Vietnam out of friendship for the United States and affirmed their belief that, despite the quarrels of the moment, that friendship would endure.[30] Nevertheless, de Gaulle's Vietnam policy was typical of his overriding concern with resisting American hegemony, and the reaction it produced from the United States was not unlike the American response to other Gaullist moves. Thus, French-American discord over Vietnam was characteristic of their relations in the 1960s.

FRANCE'S RELATIONS WITH THE VIETNAMESE

RELATIONS WITH THE SOUTH VIETNAMESE

De Gaulle's public emphasis after 1963 on a political solution based on a neutralist regime in South Vietnam produced predictable criticism from South Vietnamese leaders. Furthermore, the latter were not happy about France's decision to recognize the People's Republic of China in January 1964. In retaliation, licenses for the importation of French goods to South Vietnam were suspended, and Paris' nomination of Robert du Gardier to succeed Roger Lalouette as French ambassador to Saigon was rejected.

The French sought to dissociate themselves from the United States/ South Vietnamese contention that Hanoi had committed aggression against the South. Hence, France abstained from the communiqué adopted at the 1964 SEATO meeting which charged North Vietnam with aggression. One week later, in a speech before the French National Assembly on April 28, 1964, Couve de Murville called for application of the Geneva principles including "constitution in South Vietnam of a national and non-aligned regime until the conditions can be fulfilled for a reunification of Vietnam as a whole."[31]

The French were clearly doubtful about the ability of Diem's successor Major General Nguyen Khanh to subdue the Viet Cong so long as he remained dependent on the United States and on the American strategy of attempting a decisive military blow. In the French view, military means were inappropriate to the political problems, and dependence on the United States would further weaken Saigon's credibility at home. Thus, Khanh's predicament was not unlike that of Bao Dai: to succeed he needed to be free of the United States just as Bao Dai had required freedom from France.

The political convulsions that South Vietnam suffered after Diem's ouster led to the installation of Nguyen Cao Ky as premier on June 11, 1965. Less than two weeks later, on June 24, Ky severed diplomatic relations with France, accusing de Gaulle of "having aided directly or indirectly the enemy."[32] Diplomatic relations were not resumed until after the 1973 Vietnam cease-fire agreement.

De Gaulle's Vietnam policy challenged the legitimacy of the Saigon government. In his letter to Ho Chi Minh on February 8, 1966, he flatly stated that it should be replaced by a regime more representative of the diverse factions in South Vietnam:

Without speaking of subsequent reunification, the population of South Vietnam should be able, without external intervention, to form a representative government—which cannot, in any event, be accomplished so long as the war continues.[33]

Comments such as these led to criticism of de Gaulle in Saigon. The South Vietnamese government was itself critical, and it inspired stories in the state-controlled newspapers and sponsored public demonstrations, some of which were violent. For example, in February 1967, Saigon's Minister of Information Mai Van Dai, charged that a French-sponsored South Vietnamese government-in-exile was operating in Paris; during the week that followed there were daily demonstrations in front of the French consulate in Saigon, including one instance in which an effigy of de Gaulle was pelted with eggs. The pro-Ky groups who participated in these disturbances ostensibly protested French policy but their activities contained an implied warning to the United States. Numerous efforts to arrange peace talks were then in the offing, and apparent receptivity to these moves in Washington caused some concern in Saigon. Unable to attack the United States directly for seeking peace, the government-sponsored protests centered their attention on the French whose opposition to the Saigon government made them perfect targets.[34]

France's respect for the Saigon authorities was not enhanced as a result of the elections of September 1967, which installed a "civilian" government with Nguyen Van Thieu as president and Ky as vice-president. The voting process was ridiculed in France because several popular candidates who might have endangered a Thieu/Ky victory were not permitted to run either because they were exiled or because they were disqualified. The Saigon regime's sudden "discovery" that Au Truong Thanh, former finance minister to Premier Ky, had Communist leanings, was greeted with particular scorn in the French press.

An additional feature in the estrangement between Saigon and Paris was the presence in France of over 70,000 Vietnamese, many of whom were from the South but opposed to the Thieu/Ky leadership. These included Thanh, Bao Dai, General Khanh, and many who claimed a neutral stance in the struggle between the Saigon regime and the NLF. Not united behind any one individual or group, most Vietnamese neutralists believed that the NLF should be given some role in the South Vietnamese government, and many of them were pro-French in their orientation.[35]

The French were not concerned about their lack of communication with the Saigon authorities whom they regarded as American lackeys; after the massive infusion of American troops after 1965, the war was run by the United States. French policy assumed that American support for Saigon postponed resolution of the main issues of the fundamentally civil war.

In spite of these hostile relations with Saigon, France did not establish formal diplomatic relations with the National Liberation Front. As the Vietnam war progressed, French officials met with NLF contacts in Algiers, Phnompenh, and Peking and arranged the opening in Paris of an information office. To have gone any further would have prejudiced the final outcome of the South Vietnamese situation. Although the French advocated a new government in Saigon, they were careful not to be specific about its composition.

Even though the French granted it no formal diplomatic status, the NLF was content with de Gaulle's position, especially as expressed in the Phnompenh speech. An NLF representative later praised the speech's analysis for the following three points: the Vietnam war was a national resistance struggle; it required a political settlement; the United States would have to withdraw according to a fixed date.[36] Furthermore, in the NLF's view, the Phnompenh speech, made in an era of intense American pressure in Vietnam, required "political courage" and "integrity."[37] Finally, the NLF thought that de Gaulle's references to Algeria presented an apt comparison to the Vietnam situation. Thus, the NLF seemed fairly satisfied with de Gaulle's policy toward Vietnam.

RELATIONS BETWEEN THE FRENCH AND THE NORTH VIETNAMESE

Naturally, the positions that caused French-American estrangement and worsened relations between Paris and Saigon led to a gradual improvement in France's relations with the North Vietnamese. The sympathy for Hanoi's views expressed in France's public statements, in extraordinary private communications between French officials and those in Southeast Asia, and by improvements in the regular diplomatic channels of communication between France and North Vietnam increased French understanding of North Vietnam's policy and led to favorable North Vietnamese responses to French moves regarding the Vietnam war.

The French analysis of the conflict corresponded to that of the North Vietnamese concerning the primarily local origins of the war and the major responsibility of the United States for its escalation and continuance. The French deplored military escalation, in particular the bombing policy because of its tremendous destruction as well as its adverse effect on North Vietnam's will to negotiate. Thus, they condemned American tactics and called for an unconditional bombing pause; these moves enhanced France's prestige among Hanoi's leaders. In addition, a series of diplomatic contacts facilitated the evolution of friendly relations between the two governments.

French-North Vietnamese rapprochement was no easy feat; the North Vietnamese rightly blamed the French for facilitating American entry into Southeast Asia after the Geneva settlement, in particular, for the agreement concluded in December 1954 between French General Ely and United States General Collins transferring the function of military advisement from French to American advisers. This represented at least a violation in spirit of the Geneva proscription against the introduction of foreign troops into Vietnam. Thus, former French Foreign Minister Couve de Murville admitted ruefully, "the blame [for American entry into Vietnam] is shared by you and us."[38]

Hanoi's leaders occasionally reproached the French on this account. In his letter to de Gaulle in January 1966, Ho Chi Minh asked that France "fully assume its obligations vis-à-vis the Geneva accords,"[39] whose obligations had been abdicated with the Ely-Collins agreement. On another occasion, Ho privately reproached French Ambassador Jean Chauvel for France's failure to see that the Geneva accords were faithfully executed.[40]

Nevertheless, the North Vietnamese were gratified by French statements publicly condemning American policy in Southeast Asia, and Ho Chi Minh was willing to exploit French support for whatever its worth. Thus, his letter to de Gaulle (sent during the thirty-seven day bombing pause) included the plea that the French president "use his prestige to contribute to the hasty conclusion of all new perfidious American scheme(s) in Vietnam and in Indochina."[41] Ho did not overestimate France's ability to induce a change in American policy, but he knew that the French shared his opposition to the survival of an American military satellite regime in South Vietnam. Thus his 1966 letter to de Gaulle acknowledged some commonality in their positions.

In his reply, de Gaulle endorsed this commonality. Writing on February 8, 1966, one week after resumption of American bombing of North Vietnam, de Gaulle assured Ho that "we do not condone the prolongation of the fighting, still less its extension under the pretext of obtaining a solution."[42] Furthermore, de Gaulle presented his ideas for a settlement which were close to Hanoi's position on two counts: he denied the legitimacy of the Saigon government, and he implied criticism of American intervention in Vietnam's internal affairs. The warm tone of de Gaulle's letter to Ho contrasts sharply with the harshness *Le Monde* described as characteristic of his letter to Johnson written around the same time.

De Gaulle's correspondence with Ho Chi Minh was one of several extraordinary diplomatic contacts between the French and the Vietnamese that took place in 1965 and 1966. In addition, de Gaulle sent several personal emissaries to Asian capitals after his 1964 recognition of People's Republic of China; these included Cultural Affairs Minister André Malraux who visited Peking in July 1965, Ambassador Jean Chauvel who traveled to Peking, Hanoi, Phnompenh, and Vientiane in December 1965, and Jean Sainteny who visited Hanoi and Peking in June and July 1966.

The reports of all of these emissaries increased French pessimism regarding the chances for peace talks without an American initiative. De Gaulle's Phnompenh speech was clearly foreshadowed in an article Ambassador Chauvel wrote for *Le Figaro* on January 3, 1966, shortly after his return from Asia. Negotiations would only be possible, he wrote, "when the Americans will have admitted the futility of the operations they are pursuing. They cannot win this war. No matter how far they push it in the future, they will lose it."[43]

Malraux reported that the Chinese did not favor negotiations unless the United States commenced withdrawal from Vietnam. In addition, Malraux returned to France with the impression that the Chinese leaders were preoccupied with internal affairs. This reinforced the French view that the Chinese government was in a period of consolidation, rather than expansion.

Sainteny, who knew Ho since the two negotiated in the 1945-46 period, saw the Vietnamese leader for the last time in 1966; Ho died in September 1969. At their meeting Sainteny warned Ho concerning North Vietnam's conflict with the United States: "You're playing with fire. The United States will destroy you." Ho's reply was adamant: "we will never give up; the United States can annihilate us but they can never force us to surrender."[44] These words must have impressed de Gaulle and strengthened his conviction that the United States must seek peace through negotiations. The precondition for successful negotiations was an American decision to abandon escalation; only then would Hanoi be willing to make peace.

In late summer 1966, de Gaulle himself visited Southeast Asia. In Phnompenh, he met with Prince Sihanouk, then Cambodian head of state, Nguyen Thuong, chief of the North Vietnamese diplomatic mission in Cambodia, and Nguyen Van Hieu, foreign affairs specialist of the National Liberation Front. Sihanouk had tried to arrange a meeting with Ho Chi Minh by inviting the North Vietnamese leader to come to Phnompenh during de Gaulle's stay; Ho responded by inviting de Gaulle to come to Hanoi. De Gaulle declined this invitation; undoubtedly, the credibility of his claim to be criticizing the United States out of friendship would have been damaged by a trip to the enemy capital. Instead he chose Phnompenh as the forum from which to manifest France's solidarity with the Indochinese peoples.

Placed in the context of de Gaulle's Phnompenh talks with representatives of Hanoi and the Viet Cong and the earlier diplomatic sound-

ings of his emissaries, the Phnompenh speech reflected the French estimate of enemy demands that the United States would have to consider
if peace talks were to be arranged. De Gaulle's call for a unilateral American initiative concerning troop withdrawals represented the logical conclusion of his analysis based on American responsibility in Southeast
Asia. It also signified his progressive acceptance of North Vietnam's attitude toward the requirements for peace.[45]

The most concrete evidence of French-North Vietnamese rapprochement was the existence of regular channels of communication through
their diplomatic representation in each other's capitals. Their respective
economic missions were raised to the level of "general delegation" in
1966, and these missions constituted a continuing source of conversations between the two countries. Mai Van Bo, North Vietnam's representative in Paris from 1961 to 1970 was Hanoi's highest ranking permanent emissary in the West. His role in peace maneuvers is discussed on the
following pages.

The French moved cautiously with regard to warming their relations
with North Vietnam. Sensitive to the mistrust with which Hanoi's leaders
viewed any attempts to influence their policy, particularly on the part of
the former colonial power in Indochina, Paris was content to follow
Hanoi's lead with regard to any improvement in relations. Thus, the
French granted Hanoi's mission in Paris the status of "general delegation"
several months after the North Vietnamese raised to that status France's
mission in their capital. François Quierelle, the French delegate general
in Hanoi had conferred with North Vietnamese Premier Pham Van Dong
on several occasions before Hanoi's representative in Paris, Mai Van Bo,
met with Premier Pompidou in May 1967. The North Vietnamese sought
full diplomatic representation at the ambassadorial level during the 1960s,
but the French demurred. Prior to 1968, the French undoubtedly hesi-
tated because of their misgivings as to how the move might be interpreted
in Washington; after the start of the Paris peace talks, the French carefully
refrained from any action that might have prejudiced their position as
impartial hosts.[46] Nevertheless, in spite of French caution, the price for
French-North Vietnamese rapprochement was increased hostility toward
French policy in Washington and Saigon.

DE GAULLE AND DIPLOMATIC PEACE MANEUVERS

De Gaulle's improving relations with Hanoi and the NLF and the
simultaneous deterioration of his relations with Saigon and Washington

were natural consequences of his Vietnam policy. It can be argued that
his lack of impartiality damaged France's chances to play a mediatory
role. However, it should not be assumed that de Gaulle envisioned himself in such a capacity.

On the contrary, de Gaulle frequently denied a French intent to
mediate between the belligerents.[47] His view of the war led him to
emphasize major American responsibility and to call for a unilateral
American move to bring about peace. From this vantage point, the issues
over which the war was being fought could not be mediated. More important, prior to 1968, there seemed to be little need for mediation,
since neither of the parties appeared willing to negotiate. As de Gaulle
told Jean Sainteny, "if they don't want to settle, why should we get
involved?"[48]

In spite of these disclaimers, de Gaulle's public statements hinted at
a role for France in future peace negotiations regarding Vietnam. While
he was under no illusions about France's capacity to mediate without a
firm commitment on the part of all parties to negotiate a settlement, de
Gaulle frequently mentioned France as one of the guarantors of a peace
agreement. Also, French diplomatic contacts added to the prospects of
eventual French participation in peace talks. On the other hand, de Gaulle's
critical posture vis-à-vis United States policy and his insistence on a new
government in Saigon seriously damaged his credibility with two of the
parties in the conflict. As long as there was no common desire for negotiations, de Gaulle was content to maintain his one-sided position, well
aware of the limits it imposed on France's capacity to participate in
negotiations.

Prior to 1965, when American participation in the war deepened, the
French believed that peace talks might be possible; they hoped to prevent
further deterioration of the situation. On two occasions, in May 1964
and February 1965, France requested the reconvening of the Geneva
conference by its co-chairmen, Britain and the Soviet Union.[49] In both
cases, the idea was rejected by Britain and the United States in spite of
Soviet, Chinese, and North Vietnamese support. In July 1964, de Gaulle
lent his voice to a chorus of requests for a conference to discuss Vietnam;
the chorus included Xuan Thuy, Prince Sihanouk, Mai Van Bo, Souvanna
Phouma, and U Thant. Two days later, the Soviet Union publicly seconded
the idea. It seemed that nearly everyone concerned, including France,
sought a conference on Indochina exdept the United States and the Saigon government.

American opposition to multilateral peace talks at this time may be explained by several factors. American officials were unwilling to give the North Vietnamese/Viet Cong a forum from which to denounce publicly American policy in Southeast Asia, their denunciation seconded by the Russians, the Chinese, and the French. More fundamentally, adverse military developments and continued political instability in Saigon contributed to American reluctance to talk peace in the 1964-65 period.

Conversely, North Vietnam and its allies may have favored negotiations during the 1964-65 period for several reasons. In particular, it was to their advantage to prohibit further American bombing raids and to prevent wider American involvement in the war. The very military and political circumstances judged unfavorable from the American point of view made the moment propitious from the North Vietnamese perspective. Also, before major American escalation, it was unclear to what extent China and the Soviet Union would support the war effort. Afterwards, they undoubtedly became more militant. Thus, Chinese and Soviet approval of French efforts to bring about negotiations in 1964 and early 1965 may have indicated their lukewarm support for the war effort at that time. When American escalation led to their staunch solidarity with Hanoi and the National Liberation Front, they viewed peace talks less favorably. Their attitudes, in turn, crucially affected the prospects for negotiations: the 1973 agreements, like the 1954 Geneva accords, were made possible partially because of positive Russian and Chinese attitudes.

By mid-1965 the situation had solidified. President Johnson, in a speech at Johns Hopkins University on April 7, declared his readiness to participate in "unconditional discussions." Two weeks later, North Vietnamese Premier Pham Van Dong announced Hanoi's Four Points as conditions for peace. These included two conditions unacceptable to the United States: first, that the United States "end its policy of intervention and aggression in South Vietnam," and second, that the United States agree that South Vietnam's future should be settled in accord with the NLF's program.[50]

Thus, the public positions of the United States and North Vietnam regarding negotiations were irreconcilable, and they remained so from mid-1965 until mid-1968 when the Paris peace talks opened. The main cause, in the French view, was American escalatory action in the beginning of 1965. The first American bombing raids over North Vietnam were conducted early in February 1965 during Soviet Premier Kosygin's stay in the North Vietnamese capital. Allegedly in response to a Viet Cong attack on Pleiku twelve hours earlier, the American action was so swift and so severe as to prompt charges that the Pleiku attack was only a pretext for American escalation.[51]

The day after the Pleiku attack, William Sullivan, American ambassador to Laos, was in Paris and spoke with Etienne Manac'h, director of the Asian Division of the French Foreign Ministry. Manac'h told Sullivan how poor the timing was and warned him that the Russians could hardly ignore such American provocation and were bound to respond by giving increased aid to the North Vietnamese.[52] Soviet sympathy for peace moves diminished in proportion to American escalation. In particular, according to former French Foreign Minister Maurice Couve de Murville, the Soviets "never wanted to be in the position of supporting the Vietnamese less than did China."[53]

At a higher level, the French communicated to American officials Soviet displeasure regarding United States air attacks over North Vietnam. On Kosygin's return from Hanoi, he told French Foreign Minister Couve de Murville of his anger over the United States bombings. Shortly thereafter, Couve de Murville traveled to Washington and met with Secretary Rusk and President Johnson. Surely his conversations included some reference to Soviet sentiments.[54]

In the months that followed the initial American escalation in 1965, nothing occurred on the military or political fronts which changed de Gaulle's view of the situation or France's strategy of publicly criticizing the United States. As stated in the last section, his public stance, especially the Phnompenh speech increased the receptivity of Hanoi and the NLF to French participation in future peace negotiations.

Public postures aside, the French were involved in private diplomatic soundings which led up to the Paris peace talks. The main channel for French involvement was the regular contact in Paris between Mai Van Bo, North Vietnamese delegate general to France, and Etienne Manac'h.[55] Manac'h's understanding of the Vietnam situation and his ability to be useful were enhanced by his participation (as an aide to former Socialist Premier Guy Mollet) in contacts between General de Gaulle and the Algerian National Liberation Front prior to the settlement of the Algerian war in 1962. His views on Indochina paralleled those of de Gaulle, to whom he had direct access while he was at the Foreign Ministry. His role in the pre-conference maneuvers was not insignificant; his regular contacts with Hanoi's delegate to Paris, Mai Van Bo, and with John Gunther Dean[56] of the American embassy enabled him to aid the process whereby the two sides moved toward the conference table. Manac'h always acted on his own initiative, and he and de Gaulle understood that he was at no time to assume the post of mediator on the French government's behalf.

Mai kept Manac'h abreast of the nuances of Hanoi's position especially regarding peace talks. Occasionally, their conversations contained alleged peace feelers. For example, in May 1965, the two met during the final hours of a six-day pause in United States bombing of North Vietnam. Mai gave Manac'h a proposal which, in the main, reiterated Pham Van Dong's Four Points. It is not clear whether the report of this conversation reached Washington before the bombing was resumed; even less clear is whether it contained a serious peace offer.[57] Nevertheless, the French expressed their disappointment that the bombing was resumed after five days; they believed that the United States should have prolonged the pause and given the Communists an inducement to improve their terms.

In 1967, Mai Van Bo was involved in several reported peace feelers. First, in January, he pointedly rejected the efforts of United Nations Secretary-General U Thant to sound out the possibilities for peace talks. In the same remarks he also criticized British Foreign Secretary George Brown's call for immediate peace talks which he characterized as "the English version of the American proposal of unconditional negotiation."[58] He indicated North Vietnam's reluctance to move directly to multilateral talks in which the claims of the "aggressor" would be given equal weight with its own; in Hanoi's view, shared by the French, a successful proposal for peace must make a distinction between the aggressors and the victims.

Second, Mai repeated Pham Van Dong's remark that the Four Points were a "basis for settlement" rather than conditions for negotiations and implied that an American bombing pause could produce negotiations. Pham Van Dong spoke in an interview with Harrison Salisbury, and Mai reiterated his remarks in response to questions from newsmen in Paris. Like Pham Van Dong, Mai did not definitively state that talks would follow the bombing pause but that was the implication. This represented a modification in Hanoi's previous position.

Third, Mai was indirectly involved in another episode involving peace maneuvers. During a visit to Paris in late January 1967, Senator Robert F. Kennedy discussed the prospects for peace with Etienne Manac'h.

Manac'h's remarks seemed to contain new elements although he denied that he was transmitting a peace feeler. *Newsweek*'s account, which described the conversation as a peace move, produced a series of accusations and denials by the Johnson administration, Kennedy advisers, and French officials regarding its source.[59]

This episode was newsworthy because it occurred in the midst of continuing speculation that North Vietnam had modified its position regarding the conditions for peace talks. The private enmities between Johnson and Robert Kennedy complicated the situation, but the manner in which the Manac'h conversation was received in Washington also revealed the complete erosion of French influence among American policy makers. Regardless of the validity of the "peace feelers," Manac'h's comments might have been regarded as an informed presentation of North Vietnamese thinking. However, the Johnson administration was skeptical of reports delivered through the French because of de Gaulle's hostile policy toward American involvement in Southeast Asia. Whether or not this American reaction was justified, it severely limited the effectiveness of France's counsel.

In late February, Mai commented on reports circulating at the time of Soviet Premier Kosygin's talks in London with British Prime Minister Wilson. In a conversation with newsmen from the *New York Times* in Paris on February 22, 1967, Mai Van Bo denied rumors that Hanoi's position was about to harden after the end of a six-day bombing pause. He insisted that an American bombing halt would have to be permanent and unconditional and he said that North Vietnamese Foreign Minister Trinh's statement (in Tokyo on February 5, 1967, to Australian journalist Wilfred Burchett) that a pause "could" lead to talks represented an important "gesture of goodwill" to which the United States had responded "in bad faith."[60] Thus, the North Vietnamese expected the next move to come from the United States. The move, in the form of an American bombing pause, was to come one year later.

In the months prior to President Johnson's startling announcement of a unilateral halt in the bombing of North Vietnam, on March 31, 1968, the United States and North Vietnam had continued to move closer to negotiations through private and public signals. Among these was President Johnson's speech in San Antonio, Texas, on September 29, 1967, in which he indicated his willingness to cease the bombing if peace talks would result and if the North Vietnamese would not take advantage of the lull. The American position still emphasized some reciprocity in de-

escalatory moves prior to peace talks; in the French view this was unrealistic because the bombing represented a principle to North Vietnam
and could not be compromised. Several months later, there was some
public movement on this issue as a result of United Nations Secretary-
General Thant's soundings in several world capitals. He had made contact
with North Vietnamese emissaries at least twice: in New Delhi and in Paris
where he saw Mai Van Bo. On his return to the United States, Thant met
with Johnson and then publicly tried to reconcile the San Antonio formula with the North Vietnamese position as he knew it. In a statement
issued on February 25, 1968, Thant suggested that the United States
could reasonably assume that North Vietnam would deal in "good faith"
with the issue of ground combat if the bombing was halted. Three days
later, on February 28, the French government supported Thant's opinion
in a statement issued after the weekly cabinet meeting. At that time
Information Minister Gorse said:

U Thant's statement, according to which the unconditional halt of American bombing in North Vietnam would be a necessary and sufficient condition for the opening of peace negotiations, corresponds to information
explicitly received by the French Government.[61]

This was, to date, the most definitive statement issued by the French
government concerning peace maneuvers. It contained no French proposal
but merely confirmed information that the North Vietnamese had made
public in another context. Thus, France acted, with North Vietnamese
approval, to aid the communication flow.

Later, the French offered Paris as a site for the negotiations, a move
that ultimately broke the deadlocked discussions about a meeting place.
Paris had been mentioned during the public speculation about possible
sites but neither the United States nor North Vietnam had suggested the
French capital. On April 18, 1968, French Foreign Minister Couve de
Murville remarked that if the United States and North Vietnam agreed to
select Paris for the peace talks, "we certainly have no objection. We would,
on the contrary, be happy to make our contribution to the solution of a
difficult problem."[62] Although he denied that France was initiating a
move to break the deadlock, his action had that effect. In the words of
one American diplomat, "this speech represented a specific initiative,
though it was a carefully hedged offer."[63] On repeated occasions in the

past, the French had adamantly refused the role of mediator on the grounds that the time was not auspicious. Thus, their offer of the Paris site in 1968 must have reflected their belief that the time had come when both sides might react positively.

The Paris peace site was a compromise for both sides; while the North Vietnamese would have preferred a Communist city like Warsaw, the Americans favored a city where the climate might have been more favorable to United States policy. The choice of Paris became likely since Washington would not agree to a Communist capital and Hanoi could accept no other Western city. The French capital was acceptable to the North Vietnamese because of their large delegation there and because French policy was sympathetic to their views; the United States was willing to accept Paris as the capital of a Western ally. Naturally the Gaullist government regarded the choice of Paris as a "triumph of its policy of independence and neutrality."[64] Paris had become "neutral territory" solely as a result of de Gaulle's position on Vietnam.

De Gaulle's critical reaction to American policy in Vietnam was predictable because it coincided both with his views regarding the conflict and with his overriding foreign policy aim of expressing France's independence from the United States. Equally in character was the suspicious American response to the French president who was regarded in Washington as a perennial gadfly. South Vietnam's hostility to the French posture on Vietnam is also understandable. Conversely, de Gaulle's policy won praise among Hanoi's leaders and the Viet Cong and resulted in a partial rapprochement between France and its former Viet Minh enemies.

De Gaulle's ability to mediate between the belligerents was limited by his one-sided stance and by the unwillingness of the parties to settle. Nevertheless, France's excellent contacts with the North Vietnamese, especially through the talent and expertise of Etienne Manac'h kept the French abreast of the diplomatic movements toward the 1968 peace talks.

While de Gaulle's critical stance regarding United States policy denied him the role of mediator, it led to the selection of Paris as choice for the conference. De Gaulle was unwilling to modify his criticism in order to seek a mediatory role. In an era of relentless American military pressure against North Vietnam and French-American hostility in other quarters, de Gaulle's Vietnam policy suited both the circumstances and his foreign policy aims.

NOTES

1. Two instances in which de Gaulle's reservations about Vietnam were made
known to American officials were: first, in a conversation between French Ambassador to the United States Hervé Alphand and Secretary of State Dean Rusk on
November 13, 1961 (Department of State telegram to Saigon, No. 05790, National
Security Council Country Files, Vietnam, John F. Kennedy Library); and second,
in conversations between American embassy officials and those at the French Foreign
Office, summarized by Ambassador to France James Gavin in Department of State
telegram No. 2632 from Paris, November 18, 1961 (National Security Council
Country Files, Vietnam, John F. Kennedy Library).
2. Charles de Gaulle, *Memoires d'Espoir: Le renouveau 1955-1962* (Paris:
Libraire Plon, 1970), pp. 268-269. General de Gaulle's warning was apparently
delivered during one of four private conversations with Kennedy when only inter-
preters were present. The French president's recollections are confirmed by Kennedy's
assistants, Kenneth O'Donnell and David Powers, who accompanied him to Paris and
subsequently had access to transcripts of the Kennedy-de Gaulle meetings. (Conversations with Kenneth O'Donnell, June 24, 1975, and with David Powers, July 1,
1975, Waltham, Mass.)
3. *Chronology of the Major French Statements on Vietnam Since August,
1963* (New York: French Embassy, 1968), p. 5.
4. One forum in which criticism was raised was in the Southeast Asia Treaty
Organization (SEATO). France only sent an observer to the SEATO ministerial
meeting held in April 1965 and dissociated itself from the communiqué issued at
its close which supported the American position in Vietnam. Also, after 1967 the
French refused to participate in SEATO's joint naval maneuvers and after 1974
refused to contribute financially to the alliance. SEATO was dissolved in 1977.
5. *Le Monde*, February 18, 1966, p. 1.
6. "Speech . . . in Phnompenh, September 1, 1966," *Chronology*, p. 19.
7. Ibid., p. 20.
8. Ibid.
9. Ibid., p. 19.
10. Similarities between the two situations are discussed by Alfred Grosser, "La
Comparison Algerienne," *Le Monde*, September 4-5, 1966, pp. 1-2.
11. See *Le Monde*'s editorial of February 16, 1968, p. 1. In his book *Crisis Now*
(New York: Random House, 1968), General James M. Gavin, former ambassador
to France, suggested that the United States follow the example of de Gaulle in
Algeria and negotiate a Vietnam settlement.
12. *Chronology*, p. 34. The connection between the conflicts in the Middle
East and Southeast Asia was evoked by de Gaulle during his televised address to the
nation on August 10, 1967, and by Couve during his remarks before the United
Nations General Assembly on June 22, 1967, and September 28, 1967.
13. De Gaulle had mentioned Vietnam as an obstacle to Soviet-American coop-
eration in his remarks to the diplomatic press corps in Paris on January 1, 1967.
Foreign Minister Couve de Murville made a similar reference in an address to the
French Assembly on October 20, 1965.

14. Remarks at a Kremlin dinner honoring Premier Pompidou then visiting the Soviet Union, quoted in *New York Times,* July 4, 1967, p. 4.

15. Charles E. Bohlen, American ambassador to France from 1963 to 1968, lamented the fact that when he arrived in Paris, de Gaulle's views about Vietnam had already "crystallized" so that little real discussion between them was possible on this subject. Interview with Charles Bohlen, January 15, 1971.

16. Press Conference, July 23, 1964, *Major Addresses, Statements and Press Conferences of General Charles de Gaulle: March 17, 1964-May 16, 1967* (New York: French Embassy, 1967), vol. 2, p. 26. Furthermore, these suspicions were not confined to Southeast Asia; when the United States expressed support for de Gaulle's policy of independence for Algeria, French officials asked the United States ambassador to France, "You're not trying to replace us in Algeria, are you?" Interview with former Ambassador James M. Gavin, Cambridge, Mass., December 27, 1970.

17. This account of the Ball/de Gaulle talks may be found in Townsend Hoopes, *The Limits of Intervention* (New York: McKay, 1970), p. 28. Hoopes states that the meeting took place in December, but according to the *New York Times,* the month was June.

18. Quoted by C. L. Sulzberger, "The Dove Who Kept Cool," *New York Times,* March 12, 1971, p. 35. Under President Kennedy, at least one White House staff member considered prevailing on de Gaulle to mediate the Vietnam war. In an unsigned memorandum from President Kennedy's office files released in 1974 by the Kennedy Library, the anonymous writer advocated arranging a United States withdrawal from Vietnam in exchange for a Russian withdrawal from Cuba with de Gaulle as diplomatic broker for the trade.

19. This was the interpretation of former French Foreign Minister Maurice Couve de Murville who linked Ball's opposition to de Gaulle to the former's desire that United States influence predominate in Europe. Interview with Maurice Couve de Murville, Paris, July 6, 1972.

20. *New York Times,* March 17, 1965, p. 5. Although Ball did not mention France directly in his speech, he spoke of the "proponents of a resurgent nationalism" in Europe, and he used the phrase "from the Atlantic to the Urals" so that it was clear he meant de Gaulle.

21. President Johnson made this response in campaign speeches in Michigan and Ohio on September 5 and 6, 1966, and during his press conference on September 8, 1966. *New York Times,* September 6, 1966, p. 1, and September 8, 1966, p. 3.

22. James Reston, "Washington: The Private Maneuvers on Vietnam," *New York Times,* September 9, 1966, p. 44.

23. David Halberstam, "French Discount Letter by Rusk," *New York Times,* September 11, 1966, p. 3. The Rusk letter was neither released nor discussed publicly by American officials.

24. "Interview of Mr. Couve de Murville (Inter-Opinions)," January 7, 1967, *France and Vietnam; Major French Statements August 1963-December 1973* (New York: French Embassy, 1974), p. 33.

25. Interview with Maurice Couve de Murville, Paris, July 6, 1972.

26. Ibid.

27. John Finney, "U.S. Urged to Reveal Note to French on Peace Talks," *New York Times*, September 9, 1966, p. 1.

28. Quoted by James Reston, "Washington: The Private Maneuvers on Vietnam," *New York Times*, September 9, 1966, p. 44.

29. Lyndon Baines Johnson, *The Vantage Point* (New York: Holt, Rinehart and Winston, 1971), p. 23.

30. See, for example, de Gaulle's remarks at Phnompenh on September 1, 1966, his press conference of October 28, 1966, and the speech given before the Institute for High National Defense Studies by M. Hervé Alphand, then ambassador to the United States, on March 21, 1967.

31. *Chronology*, p. 6.

32. *New York Times*, June 25, 1965.

33. *Chronology*, p. 15.

34. The charges that France was sponsoring a Vietnamese government-in-exile originated with Mai Van Dai's brother-in-law, Brigadier General Nguyen Ngoc Loan, Chief of Military Policy. An article in Saigon's largest newspaper, *Song*, linked the United States to the rumored government-in-exile, stating it must have resulted from a French-American deal. Jonathan Randal, *New York Times*, March 6, 1967, p. 14. C. L. Sulzberger also mentions that the United States was the real target of these protests in *New York Times*, March 5, 1967, Section 4, p. 8.

35. In his first public statement after he left office in 1965, Khanh said on May 11, 1968, that the NLF should be given a role commensurate with its support at the polls. *New York Times*, May 12, 1968, p. 18.

36. Interview with Ly Van Sau, press spokesman for the NLF's delegation to the Paris peace talks, Paris, July 3, 1972.

37. Ibid.

38. Interview with Maurice Couve de Murville, Paris, July 6, 1972.

39. Quoted in *Le Monde*, February 1, 1966, p. 5.

40. The occasion was a trip to Hanoi by Chauvel in late 1966. Interview with Jean Chauvel, Paris, June 20, 1972.

41. Quoted in *Le Monde*, February 1, 1966, p. 5.

42. *Chronology*, p. 15.

43. Jean Chauvel, "Les Chances de paix au Vietnam," *Le Figaro*, January 3, 1966, p. 4. Chauvel also observed Chinese fears of a Soviet-American duopoly which explained Moscow's efforts to steer Hanoi toward a peaceful settlement. This dread of Soviet-American cooperation was shared by General de Gaulle.

44. Interview with Jean Sainteny, Paris, June 26, 1972. Sainteny related this conversation to Richard Nixon, then a private citizen whom he met for the first time in France during the summer of 1966.

45. De Gaulle's analysis was shared by his host, Prince Sihanouk and their joint communiqué reflected this accord: it emphasized the necessity of American withdrawal in accordance with the Geneva principles and of neutralization of Vietnam by international agreement. "French-Cambodian Declaration," September 2, 1966, *Chronology*, p. 21.

46. France's role as host to the Paris peace talks is discussed in Chapter 5.

47. For denials that the moment was opportune for French mediation, see

de Gaulle's press conferences on September 9, 1965, and October 28, 1966;
Foreign Minister Couve de Murville's radio interview on September 19, 1966;
and Ambassador Hervé Alphand's speech on March 27, 1967. A significant expression of France's willingness to participate in a final peace settlement appeared in
de Gaulle's letter to Ho of February 8, 1966.

48. Interview with Jean Sainteny, Paris, August 23, 1972.

49. In May 1964, French Foreign Minister Couve de Murville wrote to his
British and Soviet counterparts regarding a Cambodian suggestion that the expanded
Geneva conference be reconvened to discuss Cambodia's borders and to guarantee
its neutrality. Cambodia was at that time complaining to the United Nations regarding United States and South Vietnamese action violating its borders. In the recurrent
dispute over the boundary separating South Vietnam and Cambodia, France had
always sided with Cambodia. In February 1965, the French appeal for a reconvened
Geneva conference followed an American air response to a Viet Cong attack at
Pleiku and was contained in a statement made public on February 10. This French
move had both Soviet and North Vietnamese support. *Le Monde*, March 3, 1965
and C. L. Sulzberger's column in the *New York Times*, April 28, 1967, in which he
discusses the French proposal in retrospect.

50. Quoted in Marcus G. Raskin and Bernard B. Fall, eds., *The Viet-Nam Reader:
Articles and Documents on American Foreign Policy and the Vietnam Crisis* (New
York: Vintage Books, 1967), pp. 342-343.

51. This is the thesis of *The Politics of Escalation in Vietnam*, by Franz Schurmann, Peter Dale Scott, and Reginald Zelnick (Greenwich, Conn.: Fawcett Books,
1966). The authors contend that escalatory moves coincided with internal political
developments in Saigon and with peace overtures considered untimely in view of
the unstable situation there. See also Jean Lacouture, *Vietnam: Between Two
Truces* (New York: Vintage Books, 1966), pp. 232-233.

52. Interview with Etienne Manac'h, Paris, July 27, 1972.

53. Interview with Maurice Couve de Murville, Paris, July 6, 1972. The French
were kept abreast of the Soviet position on Vietnam by Soviet Ambassador
Vinagradov.

54. David Kraslow and Stuart H. Loory, *The Secret Search for Peace in Vietnam* (New York: Vintage Books, 1968), Part II.

55. Manac'h served as director of the Asian Division of the French Foreign
Ministry from 1960 to 1969 and as French ambassador to Peking from 1969 to
1975. See his *Memoires d'Extrême Asie* (Paris: Fayard, 1977).

56. Mr. Dean's responsibilities at the Paris embassy involved Southeast Asian
affairs. He later served as chargé d'affaires in Laos (1971-74) and as ambassador to
Cambodia (1974-75). He is currently ambassador to Denmark.

57. This "peace feeler" was first reported in the *New York Times* several months
later, on November 11, 1965, by Max Frankel and by Henry Tanner. Kraslow and
Loory discussed it in *The Secret Search*, Part II, pp. 91-160.

58. Quoted in Richard E. Mooney, "Hanoi Envoy Hints End to Bombing Could
Spur Talks," *New York Times*, January 6, 1967, p. 1.

59. According to Jean Daniel, editor of the weekly *L'Observateur*, de Gaulle
had information from sources in Hanoi that conversations could start when the

United States unconditionally stopped bombing North Vietnam. When Robert Kennedy asked de Gaulle precisely if a bombing pause might lead to talks, the French president said no, that the only thing the United States could do was to get out of Vietnam. *L'Observateur*, February 8, 1967. If Daniel's account is accurate, it is unclear why de Gaulle rejected this opportunity to act as intermediary. However, it explains Manac'h's conversation with Kennedy; forbidden by de Gaulle to pass on the new information Manac'h tried to tell Kennedy of the chances for peace talks without actually saying so.

    60. *New York Times*, February 6, 1967, p. 3, and April 28, 1967, p. 40.

    61. *Chronology*, p. 41.

    62. "Statement by Foreign Minister Couve de Murville before the National Assembly's Foreign Affairs Committee, 18 April 1968," *Chronology*, p. 43.

    63. John Gunther Dean in a telephone interview with the author, January 11, 1971.

    64. Gaullist spokesman quoted in the *New York Times*, May 4, 1968, p. 1.

Chapter 5

France and the Vietnam Peace Settlement

FRENCH-AMERICAN RAPPROCHEMENT

France's posture of hostility toward American involvement in Vietnam was no longer suitable to French foreign policy aims after the United States announced a partial bombing pause in 1968 and the two-sided Paris peace talks began.[1] The American decision to negotiate led France to change its appraisal of American intentions in Vietnam.

General de Gaulle responded positively to President Johnson's announcement of a partial pause in American bombing of North Vietnam on Sunday, March 31, 1968. On Wednesday, April 3, before the North Vietnamese reaction to Mr. Johnson's announcement was known, de Gaulle congratulated the American president for "an act of reason and of political courage."[2] As of this time, official French criticism of United States policy in Southeast Asia ceased and was never resumed with the same ferocity as before.

Thus, after 1968, the Vietnam war was no longer a contentious issue between France and the United States. De Gaulle told R. Sargent Shriver, when the latter presented his credentials as American ambassador on May 25, 1968, that differences between the two countries were "events of the moment" and that another war would find them "together again."[3] It is significant that de Gaulle spoke thusly three months before the Soviet invasion of Czechoslovakia.

In fact, the American bombing pause announced in March 1968 was the beginning of a moderate rapprochement between France and the United States which was accelerated by the events in Czechoslovakia. Clearly, the Soviet action showed the limits of de Gaulle's policy of courting Eastern Europe while putting distance between France and the United States. De Gaulle was aware of this; in an interview with C. L. Sulzberger on February 14, 1969, just two months before he resigned, de Gaulle concluded that: "There is no reason for major differences between [France and the United States] now."[4]

Another aspect of the more cordial relations between France and the United States after 1968 was the greater rapport between their leaders at the beginning of the Nixon presidency. The Johnson-de Gaulle relationship had been aggravated by de Gaulle's harsh public criticism of Johnson's Vietnam policy and Johnson's cold indifference to de Gaulle. On the other hand, de Gaulle's relations with Nixon seemed to be characterized by cordiality and mutual respect since, "with Nixon de Gaulle thought more things might be possible."[5] De Gaulle had received Nixon while the latter was out of office and the compliment was returned when the thirty-sixth United States president traveled to Europe shortly after his inauguration in 1969, stopping first and staying longest in Paris. It is probably no surprise that the two leaders got along well.

This high-level personal rapport deepened after Georges Pompidou became president of France in June 1969. The Nixon administration emphasized cooperation with America's European allies in the bilateral framework which France preferred. For instance, President Nixon conferred with European leaders individually before his trip to Peking in 1972; and, in December 1971, during his meeting with Pompidou in the Azores, he announced the devaluation of the American dollar, a move the French had long been advocating. Thus, it is with some reason that during the first years of the Nixon presidency French officials described their relations with the United States as "normally good"[6] and stressed the absence of crises between the two countries. This improved climate had some spillover effect regarding France's attitude toward United States involvement in Vietnam.

Furthermore, France's attitude toward Vietnam shifted with the changed circumstances caused by American troop withdrawals and the ongoing peace negotiations. In an era of escalating American involvement in Vietnam, the French found much to criticize in American behavior. On the other hand, an entirely different response was called for by the situation from 1968-69 until 1973 when the United States was withdrawing its ground troops and participating in negotiations to end the conflict. French demands for a bombing pause and for American troop withdrawals became superfluous as the Nixon administration implemented these two policies. Moreover, the North Vietnamese offensive in the spring of 1972 clearly placed the remaining United States troops and those of the Saigon government on the defensive. The French sympathized with the American position in these circumstances.

A crucial element in France's more favorable assessment of United States policy in Vietnam after 1968 was the conviction that the United States truly intended to extricate itself from the war. Less than one month after his meeting with President Nixon early in 1969, President de Gaulle met with his departing ambassador to Peking, Etienne Manac'h, formerly director of the Asian Division at the French Foreign Ministry. De Gaulle told Manac'h to convey to the Chinese two points: first, that the Americans had firmly decided to withdraw from Vietnam and negotiate a peace settlement, and second, that President Nixon intended to seek an improvement in United States relations with China.[7] Manac'h conveyed these thoughts directly to Chinese Prime Minister Chou En-lai on several occasions and, presumably, played some role in convincing the Chinese of their veracity.

Pompidou shared de Gaulle's belief that President Nixon intended to end United States participation in the Vietnam conflict. During a visit to the Soviet Union in October 1970 he said, "President Nixon . . . has convinced me of his desire to withdraw from Vietnam and to end the war."[8] The public expression of such sentiments by the French president in Tashkent, a Soviet city in Asia, impressed President Nixon who, by former French Foreign Minister Maurice Schumann's account, "spoke of it many times to me."[9] France's belief that the United States planned to negotiate a settlement in Vietnam explained France's failure during the period of the peace talks (1968-73) to express hostility to American actions which might have been viewed as escalatory.

The Cambodian crisis in the spring of 1970 is a case in point. The French were alarmed when Lon Nol overthrew Prince Sihanouk and when, shortly afterward, United States and South Vietnamese troops invaded Cambodia in support of the new regime. In the first place, the French were worried about their economic interests in Cambodia and, second, they were apprehensive about the widened war. Nevertheless, they refrained from any direct criticism of the United States. In September 1966 at Phnompenh, General de Gaulle had accused the United States of "increasingly extensive escalation in Asia";[10] in May 1970, a terse French statement (which referred to the "principles" of the Phnompenh address) merely regretted "that which aggravates, prolongs and widens the conflict."[11] There was no mention of who was responsible for these effects, nor was there any direct comment by the president of the French Republic. Pompidou himself did not refer publicly to the United States action until July 2, the day after American troops withdrew from Cambodia. At that time he made the following reference to his speech before the United States Congress on February 25, 1970:

> I cannot help repeating what, by the way, I have already said to the United States Congress, that is, that there will be prospects for peace in Indochina only when the United States has taken, by itself, and voluntarily, the firm resolution to evacuate Indochina.[12]

The discreet timing and mild tone of this admonition indicates the progress of French-American relations from the days when General de Gaulle was charging the United States with primary responsibility for the continuation of the Vietnam conflict. French policy no longer required the sharply critical attitude with which General de Gaulle had greeted previous escalatory moves by the United States in Indochina.

Similarly, French protests of American bombing raids over North Vietnam in 1972 were noticeably restrained. Although the French explained their reticence in terms of the discretion required of them as hosts to the peace talks, a more severe reaction might have been expected when the United States bombed targets in Hanoi itself. During one of these raids, the French diplomatic mission was damaged, and the French delegate general to North Vietnam was mortally wounded. While the French delivered a routine protest to the United States, they did not seize this occasion to object to American policy on humanitarian grounds. Such an objection need not have prejudiced the negotiations. However, it would have angered the United States, and clearly, the French were reluctant to do so. The evolution of France's attitude toward Vietnam in the years 1968-73 can only be understood in light of this new sympathy for United States policy there. France's positive estimate of the American role in

Vietnam was the result of three factors: President Johnson's decision to halt the bombing in 1968, the high degree of personal rapport between Nixon and Pompidou, and the French conviction that the United States was committed to withdraw from the conflict.

FRANCE AND THE PARIS PEACE NEGOTIATIONS

HOST TO THE PEACE TALKS

The French also tempered their earlier criticism of American policy in Southeast Asia because they believed that, as hosts to the peace talks, they were required to act impartially. This meant balancing off comments favorable to one party with remarks in which the others could take comfort. Military and political developments in Vietnam complicated the task of maintaining an evenhanded posture. Hence, French policy was not entirely acceptable to any of the four parties to the Paris talks: the United States, the Republic of (South) Vietnam, the Democratic Republic of (North) Vietnam, and the National Liberation Front which, after 1969, was called the Provisional Revolutionary Government (PRG). Conversely, each approved some elements of France's stance.

One example of impartiality was France's refusal to consider any change in the 1968 level of diplomatic representation each of the four parties maintained in Paris as long as the peace talks continued. Although the PRG was permitted to open an information office in October 1968 in accord with previous negotiations, there were no other exceptions. Hanoi's permanent representative in Paris was a delegate general (accredited to the French premier), and Saigon retained its consular representation. The United States was the only one of the four delegations to the talks that had a permanent diplomatic mission at the ambassadorial level.

The French were less successful in their efforts to provide a neutral atmosphere for the talks by limiting demonstrations protesting the war. Public manifestations against United States policy had occurred frequently in Paris during the period of major American escalation in Vietnam, and some American officials accepted the French capital as the site for the negotiations only with great reluctance. The opening of peace talks between the United States and Hanoi coincided with the outbreak of a student-worker revolt in Paris, and the French government had a double reason for frustrating public displays—reasserting its own authority domestically and providing a peaceful climate for the negotiations. Therefore,

the French invoked an old regulation of October 1935 which prohibited
street demonstrations that threatened the public order. The ban was defied
in November 1969, and the police broke up a demonstration organized
by several Leftist groups, detaining 2,651 people. From that time, demonstrations were "tolerated" although those that risked upsetting the public
order were not "authorized."[13] The Interior Ministry, which normally
would have assumed a hard line with dissenters of any sort, took the more
"liberal" position on demonstrations so as not to give political ammuni-
tion to the Communist party, the Gaullists' best organized opposition.[14]

During the four-sided negotiations which lasted from January 1969
to January 1973, the French were largely successful in confining demonstrations and rallies to indoor locations or those outside of Paris. However, occasional gatherings were noisy enough or close enough to the conference site to annoy American officials who routinely protested them.
As one American official who requested anonymity said: "Periodically,
the United States needed to remind the French of their responsibility to
remain impartial." The most important lapse in this regard occurred before
the formal signing of the cease-fire accord on January 27, 1973. A group
of noisy demonstrators, who were allowed very close to the entrance of
the old Hotel Majestic where the ceremonies were held, cheered the arrival
of the North Vietnamese and PRG contingents and booed the American
and Saigon delegations. The Paris police were quite capable of restricting
access to the sidewalks in front of the hotel as they had throughout the
four-year meetings. However, they were reluctant to use repressive measures that might give the opposition parties an issue in the legislative
elections to be held in March 1973. Naturally angered, both the American
embassy and the Saigon consulate protested this incident.

American and South Vietnamese diplomats did not regard the French
government's policy on demonstrations as the most convincing proof of
its impartial stance. Since the demonstrations were directed against them,
they would have preferred a complete prohibition. However, the French
did not attempt a total ban, for the domestic political considerations
mentioned earlier and because a more restrictive policy would have incurred the resentment of Hanoi and the PRG. Hence, the French found
it impossible to please all sides on this issue of demonstrations.

Similarly, the French were at pains to contain their public comments
on the war within the limits of impartiality. The Pompidou government
preferred to emphasize its fidelity to the policy initiated by General de

Gaulle. This was important for two reasons: first, domestically, Pompidou
was dependent on the political support of the Gaullists, and second,
France's not unimportant role as host to the talks resulted from de Gaulle's
Vietnam policy which had made Paris, capital of an American ally, acceptable to Hanoi and the NLF/PRG. It was difficult for Pompidou to deviate
from de Gaulle's Vietnam policy without bringing charges from both the
Gaullist majority and the opposition (who sympathized with Hanoi and
the PRG) that he was not being faithful to the late French president.
Nevertheless, the evolving situation in Indochina necessitated an adapta-
tion of French policy to new conditions and the Pompidou government
sought to do so while avoiding a sharp departure from the Gaullist past.

Pompidou's emphasis on continuity between his Vietnam policy and
that of de Gaulle necessarily tempered France's more positive assessment
of American policy after 1968. The French repeated their view that the
United States bore the responsibility for ending the conflict and their belief that the settlement should be consistent with what they viewed as the
political realities in Vietnam and the requisites of its future independence.
These French assessments did not always coincide with those of the United
States. Thus, while their comments may have been less harsh than previously, the French did not abandon their well-known views about the
war. In the words of Henri Froment-Meurice, chief of the French Foreign
Ministry's Asian Division: "We didn't sacrifice our character, our person-
ality, our interests."[15]

Private and public French support for a settlement more consonant
with the demands of Hanoi and the PRG than the United States or Saigon
wished prompted mistrust of France among American and South Vietnamese diplomats. "The French think they are neutral," one American
source told me, leaving no doubt that United States diplomats thought
otherwise. When asked to describe the French role in the peace negotiations, another American official said it was "to encourage Hanoi to hold
out for its demands."

Similarly, the South Vietnamese occasionally accused the French of
partisanship toward the North Vietnamese. Saigon was particularly alarmed
about the street demonstrations in Paris and was sensitive to any sign that
the French were continuing their previous policy which Saigon judged
excessively favorable to Hanoi. For example, South Vietnam objected to
a French telegram to North Vietnam on the occasion of Ho Chi Minh's
death in September 1969 in which Pompidou declared his faithfulness to

"the principles and orientation General de Gaulle gave to French policy in the Phnompenh speech."[16] A further irritating aspect of this message was Pompidou's promise that France would participate in the reconstruction of North Vietnam. The South Vietnamese found disquieting the echo of de Gaulle's Vietnam policy as well as any sign of future French friendship for North Vietnam. Hence, commenting on the telegram, South Vietnam Foreign Minister Tran Van Lam criticized France's "partisan attitude" toward the Vietnamese conflict.[17]

Ultimately, the French advocated publicly a political solution in South Vietnam similar to that suggested by the PRG. In remarks before the Foreign Affairs Committee of the French National Assembly, Foreign Minister Maurice Schumann said, on May 18, 1972:

South Vietnam ought to have an independent government, which means one including representatives of the P.R.G., of the present team and of the independent and neutralist faction.[18]

Although this statement is consistent with the earlier Gaullist argument that South Vietnam must have a regime more representative of the political spectrum than the existing government, never before had the French so clearly identified themselves with the specific proposals of the PRG.

Subsequently, the French thought better of Schumann's statement which had evidently been made without specific clearance by the president's advisers at his Elysée office and which, in the words of one knowledgeable French official, may have been "too precise." Both the United States and the Saigon representatives in Paris believed that this statement indicated continued French partiality for the Hanoi/PRG position. Also, sometime in the summer or fall of 1972, the decision was taken by Hanoi and the PRG to negotiate a settlement that would leave General Thieu in power. Thus, it would appear that French support for the coalition government idea had come too soon. Hence, in a press conference on September 21, 1972, President Pompidou declined to take a position on a three-part government and said, instead, that there were two South Vietnamese *governments* (Saigon and the PRG) and three South Vietnamese *sides* (these two plus the uncommitted or neutral side).[19]

French statements from 1968 to 1973 were not entirely pleasing to Hanoi and the PRG either. Six months prior to their espousal of the PRG's proposal for a coalition government in South Vietnam, the French supported President Thieu's claim that South Vietnam is an independent state by referring to the "four states of Indochina." President Pompidou first used this phrase on October 25, 1971, in remarks at a dinner in Paris honoring visiting Soviet Party Chairman Brezhnev. References to the four states of Indochina contrasted with previous French statements, which only named three and which upheld the Geneva principle of Vietnamese unity. This French formulation was distinct from the Hanoi and PRG position, which insisted on the country's essential unity. While not inconsistent with earlier French statements, which regarded the problem of South Vietnam's government as separate from the question of reunification,[20] it was an explicit avowal of the legitimacy of an independent South Vietnam.

Clearly the French came to terms with American reluctance to abandon its Saigon allies and with the latter's strength as they remained in power. The regime which began under the leadership of Nguyen Cao Ky and Nguyen Van Thieu in June 1965 lasted until April 1975 and thus surpassed in length that of President Ngo Dinh Diem who held power from June 1954 until November 1963. French statements immediately preceding the 1973 agreement acknowledged this staying power.

Nevertheless, the French analysis of the Indochinese situation as illustrated in French statements and actions from 1968 to 1973 corresponded precisely to neither the American nor any of the three Vietnamese views. The French were at pains to respond to the events that occurred during this period in a manner least offensive to all concerned. The fact that each of the four parties to the Paris talks subjected France to criticism at one time or another indicates France's success in maintaining an impartial stance.

FRENCH DIPLOMATIC MANEUVERS

As hosts to the negotiations, the French provided conference facilities and security for the public and some of the private meetings and offered what one French official described as good offices *"sur le plan pratique."*[21] They executed all the necessary arrangements with strict impartiality and complete discretion, to the satisfaction of all the delegations. They were particularly proud that there were no leaks regarding the private meetings between Henry Kissinger and Le Duc Tho during the two and one-half years (from August 1969 until January 1972) that they were held in

secret. French discretion in this matter was possible because the arrangements were made at the highest level and involved only a few individuals
including Jean Sainteny, former French delegate general to Hanoi, former
Foreign Minister Michel Jobert, then an aide to President Pompidou,
former Foreign Minister Maurice Schumann, and Pompidou himself.[22]

Jean Sainteny was singularly qualified to arrange the private negotiations which ultimately produced the 1973 peace agreement. During his
trip to Southeast Asia in 1966, Sainteny had met at length with his old
friend Ho Chi Minh. He came away convinced of North Vietnam's determination to resist United States intervention at all costs. Several weeks
after seeing Ho, Sainteny met for the first time with Richard Nixon, then
a private citizen who was traveling in Europe; Sainteny conveyed to Nixon
his impressions after his meetings with Ho. His acquaintance with the
future American president and his longer friendship with Henry Kissinger,
who became Nixon's chief foreign policy adviser,[23] plus his relationship
with Ho Chi Minh placed Sainteny in a unique position when the Nixon
administration assumed power.

In July 1969, Sainteny met with Nixon and Kissinger in Washington
and helped draft a letter which Nixon asked him to deliver personally to
Ho Chi Minh. However, the North Vietnamese denied him permission to
visit Hanoi, and he passed the letter to their general delegation in Paris.
Sainteny later theorized that he was not allowed to visit North Vietnam
because he would have detected Ho's failing health; the North Vietnamese
leader died shortly afterward, on September 3, 1969.

A second commission that Nixon and Kissinger gave to Sainteny was
to arrange a secret contact between Kissinger and the North Vietnamese.
Sainteny set up the first meeting in the series of private talks at his Paris
home. He emphasizes that his role was merely to bring the two sides
together after which, in his words, "I showed them where the whiskey
was and then withdrew."[24] Sainteny's frequent meetings with his Vietnamese and American friends provided him with the opportunity to
assure each of the other's credibility; however, he purposely stayed out
of the negotiations. The significance of his participation lay in arranging
the initial private contact which ultimately led to an agreement.

Officially, French diplomats, such as former Foreign Minister Maurice
Schumann and Henri Froment-Meurice, Etienne Manac'h's successor
as director of the Asian Division, operated somewhere on the pe-
riphery of the negotiating process. They held frequent conversations
with all the parties and conveyed their informed observations about the

situation without advancing any specific proposals.

The French had more frequent contacts with members of the Hanoi and PRG missions to the talks than with either the Saigon or the American delegations.[25] The American delegation kept itself at a distance from the French and insisted that the latter deal with regular embassy personnel. Nevertheless, Pompidou's high level rapport with Nixon led to important but irregular contact between Kissinger and French officials at both the French Foreign Ministry and the president's Elysée Office. The Saigon government considered French policy inimical to its interests and was less eager to confer with the French. In its view, the change in France's public stance after 1968 had not gone far enough. This did not affect France's role because the South Vietnamese, by their own admission, were not always knowledgeable about what was going on in the negotiations.[26]

The particulars of the negotiating process, especially the private talks between Kissinger and Le Duc Tho, are not known, and, hence, it is impossible to estimate precisely the degree of French participation therein. The French admit that they were not always kept informed of the progress of the private negotiations. However, their role seems to have consisted of presenting to each side their interpretation of the general bases for settlement and the particular points to which the opposite party might agree. To a very limited extent, this may have involved playing the advocate of one side before the other. However, the French emphasize that they were not "the fifth party to the negotiations."[27]

In the final days before a preliminary accord was reached in the fall of 1972, Foreign Minister Schumann conducted conversations with all concerned. He denied having played the role of mediator or messenger; rather, in his words, he was merely "present at the creation" of the preliminary accord.[28] Schumann believed that he was able to speak with some authority to both sides. The North Vietnamese knew him to be sympathetic to their cause—it was he who, in May 1972, had espoused the three-part government solution proposed by the PRG for South Vietnam. The Americans were somewhat receptive to his views, Schumann believed, because President Pompidou's faith in President Nixon's intention to withdraw from Vietnam and his public statements to that effect had won for Pompidou "a credit with Nixon."[29]

One example of Schumann's role as interlocutor occurred in July 1972 when he visited China; at that time Mao Tse-tung suggested that the PRG cease demanding Thieu's resignation. In transmitting Mao's comments to Washington, Schumann added his view that this might indicate a breakthrough.[30] Furthermore, Schumann participated in meetings with both American and North Vietnamese officials when the deadlock in the negotiations was broken in the fall of 1972. In Washington, he met with Henry Kissinger on September 22 and on the 29 with both Kissinger and Nixon. On his return to Paris, Schumann met secretly on October 6 with Le Duc Tho and with Vo Van Sung (Hanoi's delegate general in France). On October 8, according to Kissinger's public statements, the breakthrough occurred. Thus, Schumann's conversations with the concerned parties resulted in his knowledge that an accord was imminent.

Furthermore, in his talks with Nixon and Kissinger, Schumann urged a suspension of United States bombing of North Vietnam arguing that, if he were North Vietnamese, he would more readily reach an accord during a bombing pause than while the bombing continued. In his words, "the Vietnamese are a proud and courageous people who would not want it to be said that they were afraid to die. They are not afraid to die."[31] Nixon responded that he could not risk a total bombing pause at the time of the United States presidential election but that if the other side showed signs of goodwill he might halt the bombing in stages as agreement progressed. Schumann's conversations with Le Duc Tho ascertained that a partial halt was acceptable to the North Vietnamese, and he presumably conveyed this information to Washington. Thus, Schumann tried to encourage agreement between the two sides on the bombing issue.

Because he felt privy to the final negotiations, Schumann later said he and Pompidou refrained from public comment on the events of October 1972 through January 1973 when the discussions broke down and the United States engaged in intensive bombing of North Vietnam. According to Schumann, the French did not wish to jeopardize a delicate situation that they believed would ultimately result in agreement. Nevertheless, President Pompidou did express his personal regrets about the resumed bombing in a secret letter to President Nixon a few days after Christmas 1972.

In the final analysis, this role of interlocutor for the parties to the peace conference seems to have fulfilled French expectations. The discretion with which they acted throughout the five years of the conference reflected their realization of the limitations under which they operated. Some American officials remained unconvinced of a change in France's position despite Pompidou's sympathetic view of United States policy in Asia; Saigon's diplomats shared this skepticism. The French were necessarily prudent with all three Vietnamese delegations lest they be charged with neo-colonialism. Finally, the French were unable to be effective (and therefore reluctant to act) in the absence of a willingness to settle on the part of all the parties.

POSTWAR FRENCH DIPLOMATIC POLICY IN VIETNAM

French policy after the 1973 accords resembled France's efforts immediately after the 1954 Geneva accords. In both cases, France initially attempted to maintain cordial relations with both Vietnamese regimes. In 1954, French neutrality was abandoned because of France's dependence on the United States and the latter's strong support of Ngo Dinh Diem and because of French economic interests in the South. These interests were also important in 1973, and they caused a slight tilt toward Saigon in France's Vietnam policy. However, the French also sought to keep their lines to Hanoi open and to preserve as far as possible the neutral stance adopted during the peace talks.

The 1973 French policy essentially bided time until the outcome of the military-political situation in Vietnam became clearer. Thus, shortly after the Paris accords were signed France announced its intention to send ambassadors to Hanoi and Saigon. Significantly, the PRG's status remained unchanged. Furthermore, renewing full diplomatic representation was a French overture to the Thieu regime because it was done on France's initiative whereas the 1965 break in relations had been originated by Saigon.

Hanoi and the PRG were understandably displeased with France's action. In their view, a prudent French policy would insist upon fulfillment of the terms of the 1973 accords dealing with the establishment of a new government in South Vietnam; instead, the French lent recognition to one of the two contending regimes. The North Vietnamese twice previously had cause to reproach France for not living up to its international commitments. Although the French were not committed to the 1973 agreements as directly as they were to those concluded in 1946 or 1954, or as capable of influencing the situation, they might have chosen to await future events before renaming an ambassador to Saigon. Instead, they gave the Saigon regime the right to declare that the PRG "is nothing to France but a group representing a political view . . . (with) no official status."[32]

The French defended their action by explaining that they recognize states, not regimes.[33] On a more practical level, they seem to have concluded that the Paris accords left the Saigon government in power until such time as elections were held to form a successor. Therefore, the regime in power in Saigon was a fact to be dealt with. This argument was unacceptable to the North Vietnamese on two counts: first, they have always claimed that there is only one Vietnamese state and, second, in their interpretation, the 1973 accords recognized the existence of two governments in South Vietnam. By the latter reasoning, France should also have recognized the PRG. The French did not offer the PRG full diplomatic representation until May 14, 1975, that is, after the Hanoi/PRG victory in South Vietnam, in spite of the fact that some French enterprises were in areas which the PRG already controlled in January 1973.

One explanation for this French policy is that the pressures on France to improve its relations with the Saigon government were persuasive. France and South Vietnam were potentially important trading partners. The figures (in millions of francs) for 1960, 1968, and 1972 are as follows.[34]

	1960	1968	1972
French Exports to South Vietnam	223	90	166
French Imports from South Vietnam	170	35	30

The sharp decrease after 1960 was a result of the war, which inhibited the operation of South Vietnam's rubber plantations, and the restrictions on trade with France set by the Saigon government in 1964, which were lifted in 1969, resulting in a slight increase of South Vietnamese purchases of French goods. Continued fighting kept the figure of South Vietnamese sales to France low. Also, French sales to Saigon fell off as a result of the United States role as key supplier to South Vietnam.

Nevertheless, prior to the 1973 accords, French economic interests in South Vietnam remained important. In 1972, France ranked fifth as a supplier of South Vietnam and second as a destination for exported Vietnamese goods. French sales to South Vietnam represented 5.6 percent of the latter's foreign purchases (after 46 percent from the United States, 19 percent from Singapore, 18 percent from Japan, and 6 percent from Taiwan). France received 25 percent of South Vietnam's total sales abroad, after 35 percent which went to Japan; Japan replaced France as South Vietnam's number one customer in 1972.

Furthermore, private French investment constituted a very important factor in the South Vietnamese economy. French companies maintained a near-monopoly in terms of ownership of private enterprise. Neither the Vietnamese themselves nor other foreigners owned a considerable portion of the Vietnamese economy. Private American investment was practically nil. Most important among French-owned enterprises in South Vietnam were the rubber plantations which yielded South Vietnam's main product. Eight societies owned by French interests accounted for 90 percent of all the rubber production in South Vietnam and 95 percent of all its rubber exports.[35]

In the industrial sector, the French had substantial holdings in the production of tobacco, matches, beverages, shoes, soft drinks, liquid gas, tires, building materials, mechanical engineering, automobiles, public works and civil engineering projects, and pharmaceuticals. Financially, the French were also important; three French banks (two subsidiaries of the Banque d'Indochine and the Banque Nationale de Paris) accounted for 17 percent of financial activity and retained 19 percent of the deposits. In the area of transport, Air France and Union des Transports Aerienne (UTA) handled almost all the air traffic between Vietnam and Europe and an important part of that between Saigon and other Asian cities. Moreover, French shipping nearly monopolized Saigon-Europe traffic and, interestingly, handled 35 percent of the traffic between the United States and Saigon.[36] It is remarkable that French economic interests persisted in South Vietnam nineteen years after the Geneva accords ended France's colonial domination there and despite massive American involvement in the country's affairs.

French hopes to retain an important place in South Vietnam's economic life were based on several assumptions. The French argued that it was desirable from South Vietnam's viewpoint to maintain links with France in the commercial and financial area in order to diversify its foreign investors and customers. (The French made the same argument with respect to North Vietnam.) Furthermore, the French hoped that past ties, including habits of buying French goods of a certain quality, the positive orientation of French-trained elites, etc. would induce the Saigon government to favor sustained or increased dealings with France.[37]

In June 1973, the French dispatched to Vietnam an exploratory mission headed by Gaullist legislator François Missoffe to report on future economic cooperation between France and Vietnam.[38] Based on his report, the French and the South Vietnamese signed an agreement on December 6, 1973, whereby France would supply 100 million francs in economic assistance to South Vietnam. This French decision coincided with France's goal to increase trade with Asia in the 1970s.[39]

Thus, immediately following the 1973 accords, French business interests seemed to have the most to gain from a policy in support of the Thieu regime. These business interests do not determine France's foreign policy but they are not without influence in French politics. "While one cannot yet speak of a lobby," one French official told me in 1973, "there are strong pressures from interests in France who wish to resume and replenish French commerce with Indochina." The late President Pompidou, himself a banker, was probably more receptive to the needs of this business community than General de Gaulle, whose foreign policy had a dynamism of its own. Some of the companies with interests in Vietnam, such as Michelin, were very powerful. Furthermore, there was that intangible but important network of ties between government and business which is always a crucial factor in French political life. The father of French President Valéry Giscard d'Estaing was a director of one of the large companies with interests in Vietnam. The late father of Tessier du Cros, an expert on Asian economic affairs in the French Foreign Ministry who accompanied Missoffe to Vietnam in June 1973, served on the board of another. Hence, the influence of the business community on France's policy toward Vietnam in 1973 was not negligible.

In contrast, the prospects for increased economic contacts with North Vietnam differed radically from the South Vietnamese picture. After the French defeat in 1954, the North Vietnamese confiscated all of the considerable industrial interests in French hands and trade between the two countries shrunk. In the 1960s, due partly to the wartime conditions in North Vietnam, its trade with France totaled only around $500,000 annually. The commercial agreements that the two countries had signed every year since 1955 were not renewed in 1971 but were replaced by a vague agreement that did not itemize preferential products or mention specific arrangements to encourage commercial exchanges. Also, in the period immediately prior to the 1973 accords, several proposed French projects of technical assistance to North Vietnam fell through because the financial terms were not favorable enough to the North Vietnamese. Any French hopes for increased trade with Hanoi rested on France's ability to supply North Vietnam with aid to finance North Vietnamese imports of French goods. Accordingly, on December 22, 1973, a French-

North Vietnamese agreement was signed which provided for French aid totaling 100 million francs or the identical amount to that awarded South Vietnam. Thus, the French tried to retain the possibility of improved future relations with Hanoi in the uncertain period after the 1973 accords and the American withdrawal from Vietnam.

The victory of the Hanoi/PRG forces in 1975 and the subsequent unification of Vietnam one year later necessitated a new French policy. Predictably, the new authorities in South Vietnam froze all private French assets in 1975. This ban was partially lifted in April 1977 after Vietnam's Premier Pham Van Dong made a state visit to France. The visit was significant for two reasons: first, it indicated that the Vietnamese were willing to exploit possible sources of aid other than the Soviet Union and China, and second, the French promise of 671 million francs in aid to Vietnam was a favorable French response. A further result of the visit was an agreement to allow a French company, Elf-Aquitaine, certain oil exploration rights in Vietnam. These tentative moves do not permit a firm prediction regarding future relations between France and Vietnam. Undoubtedly, Hanoi's future attitude toward private enterprise in Vietnam and France's willingness to extend economic aid are the key variables.

During and immediately after the five-year Paris negotiations on Vietnam, France successfully pursued a flexible policy that responded to changing military and political circumstances. This policy entailed significant modifications in France's relations with the United States, North Vietnam, South Vietnam, and the PRG. In particular, the French became more sympathetic to American policy in Vietnam after 1968 when they believed that the United States truly intended to withdraw from Vietnam. Furthermore, France's position as host to the five-year peace negotiations imposed restrictions on French policy. After 1968, de Gaulle and Pompidou refrained from public positions that might alienate any of the four delegations to the talks. Their response to events in Indochina was more muted than earlier French comments and displayed a higher degree of flexibility. The French were ultimately successful in maintaining a more or less balanced position and their conversations with all the parties involved them in the negotiating process. Finally, after the peace settlement, France attempted a course in Vietnam that would maximize its options. In the same spirit of neutrality that was adopted during the peace negotiations, France extended full diplomatic representation and economic aid in equal amounts to North and South Vietnam. This evenhanded policy seemed

suited to the unresolved military and political situation in Vietnam and
to France's desire for flexibility during the post-1973 period. The altered
situation after 1975 necessitated a further modification of French policy.
The future direction of France's relations with Vietnam cannot be pre-
dicted with certainty.

NOTES

1. An earlier version of this chapter appeared in *Political Science Quarterly*
89 (June 1974), pp. 305-324. Reprinted by permission.

2. "Statement at the close of the cabinet meeting on April 3, 1968," *Chronology
of the Major French Statements on Vietnam since August, 1963* (New York: French
Embassy, 1968), p. 41. De Gaulle himself had no knowledge of the North Vietnamese
reaction, according to *Le Monde*'s diplomatic correspondent Maurice Delarue.

3. *New York Times*, May 26, 1968, p. 43.

4. *New York Times*, November 11, 1970, p. 18.

5. Interview with René de Saint Legier, Paris, July 5, 1972. M. the Marquis de
Saint Legier de La Sausaye was director of the American Division at the French Foreign Ministry from 1972 to 1975 and was General de Gaulle's diplomatic counselor
from 1964 to 1969.

6. Ibid.

7. An account of de Gaulle's meeting with Manac'h is given by James Reston in
the *New York Times*, August 1, 1971, p. 11E. Reston's version was confirmed by
Ambassador Manac'h in an interview in Paris, July 27, 1972.

8. *La France et Le Vietnam: Recueil des Principales Declarations Francaises,
Août 1963-Novembre 1971* (New York: French Embassy, 1972), p. 110.

9. Interview with Maurice Schumann, Paris, July 6, 1973.

10. "Speech by General de Gaulle in Pnompenh, September 1, 1966," *Chronology*,
p. 20.

11. "Communiqué des Ministère des Affaires Etrangères (Intervention Americano/
sud-vietnamienne au Cambodge), 1 mai 1970," *La France et le Vietnam*, p. 93.

12. Press Conference, July 2, 1970 (New York: French Embassy, 1970), p. 13.

13. This is the explanation I received July 1972 from the press section of the
French Foreign Ministry in Paris. French officials were understandably reluctant
to discuss this policy.

14. The leader of the French Communist party, George Marchais, occasionally
chided Pompidou for not remaining faithful to de Gaulle's policy regarding Vietnam.

15. Interview with Henri Froment-Meurice, Paris, July 4, 1973.

16. *Le Monde*, September 20, 1969, p. 7.

17. *Le Monde*, October 4, 1969.

18. "Communiqué de La Commission des Affaires Etrangères de l'Assemblée
Nationale," *La France et Le Vietnam Août 1963-Juin 1973* (Paris: Ministère des
Affaires Etrangère, 1973), p. 46.

19. "Excerpts on Foreign Policy from the Press Conference by Georges Pompidou,
President of the French Republic at the Elysée Palace, September 21, 1972" (New
York: French Embassy, 1972), p. 7.

20. See, for example, de Gaulle's letter to Ho Chi Minh of February 8, 1966.

21. Interview with Michel Rouganou, deputy director, Press Office, Bureau de la Presidence de la République, Paris, June 22, 1972.

22. The process by which initial secret contact between Americans and North Vietnamese was arranged by Jean Sainteny, a private French citizen, is described on page 124. One month after the first meeting in August 1969, Kissinger met French Foreign Minister Schumann in New York and requested the cooperation of the French government in the logistical arrangements surrounding future meetings. Former Foreign Minister Schumann described this, his first meeting with Kissinger (and with President Nixon), in an interview in Paris on July 6, 1973.

23. Sainteny had met Kissinger several years previously when Madame Sainteny was a summer student at Harvard.

24. Interview with Jean Sainteny, Paris, June 26, 1972.

25. One American official spoke scornfully of Madame Binh, the PRG's chief delegate, who rushed to the French Foreign Ministry whenever anything disturbed her.

26. Interview with Nguyen Trieu Dan, spokesman for the Saigon delegation to the peace talks, Paris, July 5, 1973.

27. Interview with Henri Froment-Meurice, Paris, July 4, 1973.

28. Schumann's claim, in a statement in January 1973 that the French had made two specific suggestions to advance the negotiations, was exaggerated. When I spoke with him in July 1973, he gave a much more modest account of his role.

29. Except for references to Tad Szulc's account of the negotiations the preceding and succeeding description of Schumann's role is based on an interview with him in Paris on July 6, 1973.

30. Tad Szulc, "Behind the Vietnam Cease-Fire Agreement," *Foreign Policy* (Summer 1974), p. 45.

31. Ibid., pp. 54-55.

32. Interview with Nguyen Trieu Dan, spokesman for the Saigon delegation to the Paris peace talks, July 5, 1973.

33. By the same reasoning France, like the Soviet Union, maintained its ties with the Lon Nol government which ousted Sihanouk in 1970 and ruled Cambodia until 1975.

34. French Foreign Ministry, Economic Section and Centre National du Commerce Exterieur, a quasi-governmental organization based in Paris.

35. Interview with Jacques Mer, a French Foreign Ministry official occupied with France's economic relations with Indochina, in Paris, July 9, 1973.

36. Ibid.

37. Ibid. Also, interview with Madame Marte Parent, an official at the Direction des Relations Economiques Exterieurs of the French Finance Ministry, July 1973.

38. M. Missoffe has had varied experience in Asia. As a young lieutenant in 1945, he was attached to the China-based mission directed by Jean Sainteny, whose aim was to restore French authority to Indochina as quickly as possible. Later, he served as France's ambassador to Japan from 1964 to 1966.

39. President Pompidou's trip to China in September 1973 was also important in this regard.

Conclusion

France's Vietnam Policy Assessed

A country's foreign policy in any one regard is a product of many factors including the following: its overall foreign policy goals and tactics; historical influences; and the circumstances of the immediate situation. France's response to American policy in Vietnam was a manifestation of Gaullist foreign policy, of historical quarrels between France and the United States over Indochina, and of the evolving situation in Vietnam.

RELATIONAL FACTORS

Like that of his predecessors, Charles de Gaulle's foreign policy was preoccupied with France's relationship with the United States. All of France's leaders after 1944 were profoundly aware of the contrast between France's loss of status and the preeminent position held by the United States. This issue was sensitive during the immediate postwar period when the effects of the war, defeat, and occupation were fresh; it was even more crucial during the 1960s when France had recovered from the war's devastation and sought to reassert some degree of influence on continental and global affairs. To de Gaulle's consternation, the United States was becoming even more powerful during this period and, in his view, American leaders arbitrarily refused to share political decisions with a recovered France.

   The late French president strongly resented American dominance of
its allies and the United States tendency to equate alliance interests with
its own. De Gaulle's response was to continue the development of an
independent French nuclear force, to eliminate French participation in
NATO, and to reserve for France the judgment as to when to honor its
commitment under the North Atlantic Treaty. Unable to increase French
influence over American policy (both within NATO and beyond), de
Gaulle sought to dissociate France from the United States. During the mid-
1960s his determination to express France's independence from the
United States had evolved to include opposition to the overwhelming
American predominance in world affairs and the dangerous American will
to hegemony. His criticism of United States policy in Vietnam was a manifestation of these concerns. Furthermore, this emphasis on an independent
French foreign policy has been continued by de Gaulle's successors.

   In addition to its direct relationship to his policy toward the United
States, de Gaulle's attitude toward Vietnam paralleled his attempt to continue France's global role. While relations with the United States and
Europe remained paramount, de Gaulle clearly believed that France was
not merely a continental power. After the Algerian war was settled in 1962
and because of a stalemate in his European and Atlantic policies, de
Gaulle attempted to increase France's popularity in the Third World. His
criticism of United States policy in Vietnam served this end. Furthermore,
the Fifth Republic's foreign policy depended on hastening modification
of the strict bipolarity which, in the late 1940s and 1950s, restricted
France's opportunities in foreign policy. The French posture in Vietnam
was related to this French preference for international fluidity. France's
recognition of China and its emphasis on the local origins of the Vietnamese struggle testified to the diversity in the Communist world that
was characteristic of the 1960s and that de Gaulle sought to hasten.
Third World countries shared France's preference for this looseness in
international relations and, in this regard, de Gaulle's Vietnam posture
augmented French prestige in the less developed world.

   De Gaulle's comments on international crisis situations, such as the
1967 Arab-Israeli war, might possibly have led to a French mediatory
role. However, his pro-Arab stance did not enhance his credentials as
honest broker, although it may have increased his popularity among an
important segment of Third World nations.

   In some respects the Middle Eastern and Vietnamese situations paralleled each other. In Vietnam, as in the Middle East, de Gaulle was convinced that there could be no mediation between aggressor and victim. Preferring partisanship to neutrality, he cast his support behind North Vietnam whom he considered the aggrieved party and charged the United States with major responsibility for expanding and continuing the war. This increased his popularity in Hanoi and among the Viet Cong but did not qualify him to mediate. Thus, in both the Middle East and Vietnam situations de Gaulle's strong views caused him to shun a neutral posture. Furthermore, in both cases, great power interests and situational circumstances (chiefly, the unwillingness of the parties to settle) combined in a manner unfavorable to the exercise of French influence.

Therefore, the Fifth Republic's Vietnam position can be partially understood in relation to the other aspects of French foreign policy, chiefly, the predominant concern of France's leaders with its relationship to the United States and de Gaulle's insistence on a global role. American misconduct in Vietnam was an ideal target for French criticism that would express France's independent foreign policy and its global interests.

HISTORICAL FACTORS

Equally as important as the overall aims of de Gaulle's foreign policy in determining France's Vietnam stance were the historical differences between France and the United States regarding Indochina. De Gaulle did not invent French-American hostility; neither did he originate French disapproval of United States policy in Southeast Asia. Rather, the differences between the allies over Vietnam in the 1960s continued an argument which had begun twenty years earlier. Moreover, discord over Vietnam concerned the basic question of French-American relations in the post-World War II period when ascending American power assumed responsibilities that once belonged to (the now declining) France.

An antecedent of de Gaulle's Indochina policy lay in the tension between him and Franklin Roosevelt, especially the latter's hostility to the reassertion of French authority in Indochina after World War II. The American president's belief that the French defeat in 1940 disqualified France from retaining control of its Far Eastern colonies was well known, and the delayed return of French troops to Indochina—which enabled Ho Chi Minh to gain additional prestige—can be partially attributed to United States action. The United States decision to condone France's resumption of control in Indochina, contained in a statement by President Roosevelt on April 3, 1945, was belated, in French eyes.

The French were subsequently dissatisfied with the degree of American support for their struggle against the Viet Minh from 1946 to 1954. American economic and military aid to the French forces in Indochina was announced by Secretary of State Dean Acheson in May 1950, not coincidentally, five months after the Communist victory in China. From 1950 to 1954 the United States bore an increasing share of the war's costs for the purpose of preventing a Communist takeover in Vietnam. This American goal was only temporarily served by maintaining a French presence and American officials intermittently pressured the French to permit the South Vietnamese government a greater degree of independence as a means of countering the Viet Minh's anti-colonialist appeal.

In contrast, despite their anti-Communist rhetoric, the French fought in Indochina for the sole purpose of restoring their authority in the peninsula, that is, in futile opposition to their declining post-World War II position. They resisted American pressure to increase South Vietnam's independence in which they detected American ambivalence toward France's continued role in Vietnam. Moreover, they distrusted American motives and believed that the United States sought to usurp France's place in Indochina. Thus, in the 1945-46 period when the French returned to Vietnam and throughout the French-Viet Minh struggle from 1946 to 1954, the policies of France and the United States were not mutually reinforcing.

The basic differences between the allies surfaced in 1954, when France, realizing it could not retain its Vietnamese colony, sought a negotiated settlement; this French decision was not supported by the United States. On the contrary, American officials blamed the French for ceding the northern half of Vietnam to the Communists. In a sense, neither of the two countries dealt effectively with the realities of a situation in which the nationalist and Communist forces were one. At Geneva, the French acknowledged the necessity of dealing with Ho Chi Minh but they minimized the importance of his ideology and of its effects on eventual reunification of the two Vietnamese regimes. With few alternatives, the French delegation accepted the best terms it could arrange with the Viet Minh through the good offices of Soviet Foreign Minister Molotov and British Foreign Minister Eden. The United States provided little diplomatic assistance and kept its distance from the Geneva accords themselves.

French-American disagreements continued in the 1954-56 period when remaining French troops were withdrawn and the United States assumed the task of advising the South Vietnamese militarily.

The United States did not learn the lessons of France's seven and one-half year struggle to retain its colony: that, to survive, an anti-Communist régime in Vietnam must be able to tolerate internal criticism, to withstand pressure from Hanoi, and to act independently. These lessons were not lost on the French.

From his exile in Columbéy-les-deux-églises, de Gaulle observed the events of 1946-54, and his views on subsequent American involvement in Vietnam were influenced by the Fourth Republic's experiences in Indochina and by his own in Algeria. His contact with the forces of anti-colonial nationalism in Algeria and his assessment of Vietnamese politics determined his view that the struggles in South Vietnam during the 1960s, like those of the 1950s, were political in character and internal in origin.

According to de Gaulle's interpretation, military means would never resolve the essentially political problems facing the Vietnamese and he urged a halt to the expanding involvement of American military power. Fearful of the dangers of unrestricted escalation and conscious of the possibility that France might become involved in an expanded war, he advocated a negotiated settlement. His evaluation of North Vietnamese (and Chinese) intentions led him to conclude that an unconditional bombing halt and an American resolution to withdraw from Vietnam were the only measures that would bring about successful negotiations. His conviction that American policy was inappropriate to the circumstances in Vietnam was shared by most elements of political and public opinion in France.

French officials offered a perspective distinct from the American view during the Laotian crisis of 1960-62. Other antecedents of the public differences between France and the United States regarding Vietnam in the mid-1960s were the events in Saigon during 1963, when, once again, United States policy moved in directions contrary to French aims. Specifically, the overthrow of Ngo Dinh Diem eliminated the chances of a resurgence of French influence in South Vietnam at the moment when rapprochement between Paris and Saigon seemed possible.

Thus, from a historical point of view French-American discord over Vietnam in the 1960s was practically inevitable. Given the suspicion aroused in France of American motives in Indochina after 1940, French leaders in the 1960s—regardless of their personal feelings or political philosophies—could not help but resent the American role in Vietnam. Indeed, American policy makers themselves viewed de Gaulle's criticism of United States policy in Vietnam in historical perspective: they believed it was rooted in French bitterness over losing the first Indochina war. Undoubtedly, these bitter feelings existed but they were accompanied by the conviction that the forces of national liberation could not be suppressed. Thus, American policy makers assumed that an American success in Vietnam was unacceptable to the French, whereas, in the French view, an American victory was simply not possible.

Furthermore, each country viewed the actions of the other in the 1960s as a reinforcement of previous positions: United States officials believed French criticism of American policy in Vietnam was true to form, and the French thought that American policy in the 1960s regarding Southeast Asia was as misguided as it was in the 1940s and 1950s. Events in the first years of the Fifth Republic in Laos and South Vietnam reinforced France's conviction that United States policy in that area was misguided and contrary to French interests. Thus, when added to the relational factors discussed earlier—de Gaulle's predominant concern to express independence from the United States and to exhibit France's global interests—the historical circumstances made the opportunity to criticize United States policy in Vietnam irresistible.

SITUATIONAL FACTORS

France's general resentment of the United States after World War II and its previous differences with American policy in Indochina preceded French opposition to American policy during the 1960s. However, French policy was also determined by the shifting circumstances in Vietnam.

During increasing direct American military involvement in Vietnam, especially after 1965, the French severely criticized United States policy, culminating in de Gaulle's speech at Phnompenh on September 1, 1966, when he urged the United States unilaterally to announce a schedule for its withdrawal from Vietnam.

Undoubtedly, the virtues of this course were more apparent to French policy makers than to those in Washington. De Gaulle believed that French interests would best be served by promoting stability in Indochina through its neutralization from great power conflict, a solution that might have permitted a limited reassertion of French influence in the area. From the

American point of view, the benefits of United States withdrawal were less clear, and some American officials regarded de Gaulle's September 1966 speech as evidence that he was pursuing goals contradictory to those of the United States.

De Gaulle's well-known views on Vietnam, which were frequently conveyed in private prior to public statements, were not well received in Washington for two reasons. First, the United States government was not very receptive to criticism of its Vietnam policy, particularly if the suggested solution involved neutralization. Second, de Gaulle's position on Vietnam was regarded in Washington as a further manifestation of his troublesome character and chronic anti-Americanism; in Washington's view, de Gaulle was not to be taken seriously.

De Gaulle's tactics encouraged this American assessment. His acerbic public criticism of United States policy in Vietnam reflected his deeper aim—opposing American hegemony—and paralleled his negative response toward United States policy in other contexts. His Vietnam stance added to the layer of resentment that inhibited communication between France and the United States. On the other hand, American disregard of French advice on Vietnam confirmed de Gaulle's conviction that the United States was arrogant and unresponsive to allied interests. Thus, the Vietnam issue fueled the mutual hostility between France and the United States in the 1960s.

France's relations with the Vietnamese varied directly with its inharmonious ties with the United States. The Saigon government was naturally hostile to French policy; this did not upset the French because of their conviction that Saigon was Washington's puppet. In contrast, the North Vietnamese and Viet Cong approved of French criticism of United States actions in Vietnam, although they were probably under few illusions regarding France's power to influence the situation. Rapprochement with Hanoi and the Viet Cong enabled French officials to keep informed of progress toward negotiations and facilitated the choice of Paris as site for the peace talks.

France's policy toward Vietnam during the 1968-73 Paris peace talks contrasted with its earlier stance. In the year before his resignation from the French presidency in April 1969, General de Gaulle himself inaugurated this new French policy which had three aspects: a more favorable assessment of United States actions in Vietnam; a neutral attitude befitting the host to the ongoing negotiations; and a diplomatic role among the conference participants.

The French believed, as President Pompidou often stated, that the United States truly intended to extricate itself from Vietnam. Furthermore, France's favorable assessment of United States intentions in Vietnam was part of a general improvement in relations between the two countries after 1968. In March, President Johnson announced the first de-escalatory American move in Vietnam since 1963, and in August, Soviet troops invaded Czechoslovakia. The latter recalled the Soviet threat and mandated alliance solidarity.

France's neutral stance during the peace talks was not always satisfactory to all sides. In particular, the American and Saigon delegations often objected to the public demonstrations against them which were tolerated by the French government. On the other hand, the Hanoi and NLF/PRG delegations were not happy with France's failure to criticize obvious American escalatory moves, such as the 1970 invasion of Cambodia.

France's contacts with all the delegations enabled French officials to participate peripherally in the talks. A private French citizen, Jean Sainteny, set up the private Kissinger-Le Duc Tho contacts, and officials, such as Foreign Minister Maurice Schumann, were sometimes privy to the negotiating postures. Nevertheless, the French mediatory function was limited because there were other interlocutors available (that is, the Soviet Union and China) and because the parties could negotiate directly with one another.

After the 1973 cease-fire accord, the French attempted to continue the neutral stance adopted during the peace talks so as to keep open future options. Confiscation of private French assets in 1975 repeated the action Hanoi had taken in North Vietnam after its 1954 victory. It is not clear whether the Hanoi government will relent on its attitude toward private property so as to favor the French economic interests which were so important in Vietnam's past. Future French policy will be influenced strongly by this issue.

Thus, French policy toward Vietnam varied with the situational circumstances. In the period of military escalation and heightening American involvement, the French, influenced by their past disagreements with the United States over Indochina and by French-American conflicts in NATO and elsewhere, were strongly critical of United States policy in Vietnam. Their criticism reflected French convictions about the erroneous course being pursued by the United States in Vietnam and also served de Gaulle's foreign policy ends. However, in the period after 1968 when the Paris negotiations in Vietnam were in progress and American involvement in

Vietnam was declining, French policy shifted to a more neutral stance. This new French posture suited the new friendliness in French-American relations as well as France's position as host to the talks and its hopes for a future role in Vietnam. Thus, French policy exhibited some flexibility in responding to a dynamic situation; this situational flux is the final element in a French strategy that was internally consistent with its foreign policy goals and historically predictable.

The long duration of French-American discord over Vietnam relates to its basic causes: the nature of the alliance relationship between an ascending superpower and a declining middle power. Such relations are never easy. When they involve an area where superpower military involvement has replaced middle power dominance, they become especially sensitive. The middle power is simply unable to affect a situation now dominated by its senior ally; this impotence is frustrating as is the fact that the only possible response is ineffective criticism of its ally's conduct. The magnitude and style of the protest is affected by the character and status of a country's leaders. Clearly, General de Gaulle was more suited than either his predecessors or his successors in personal temperament and political circumstance to mount such a critique of American policy. However, his Vietnam policy was not merely a product of his personal philosophy of statecraft. In its historical antecedents and its preoccupation with the France-United States relationship, it reiterated a basic concern of postwar French foreign policy. Furthermore, French-American relations are likely to remain of central importance to France as it continues to adjust to middle power status. The enormity of American resources in comparison to those of France as well as the unique national perspective each country has exhibited in many areas including Indochina since 1940 indicate that discord between them is likely to persist.

Bibliography

OFFICIAL DOCUMENTS AND PUBLICATIONS

France. La Documentation Francaise. *La Politique de Cooperation avec Les Pays en Voie de Developpement* Rapport Jeanneney. Paris, 1964.

———. Ministère des Affaires Etrangères. *La France et Le Vietnam Recueil des principales déclarations françaises Août 1963-Novembre 1971*. Paris, 1972.

———. *La France et Le Vietnam Recueil des principales déclarations françaises Août 1963-Juin 1973*. Paris, 1973.

French Embassy. Press and Information Division. *Chronology of The Major French Statements on Vietnam Since August 1963*. New York, 1968.

———. *Excerpts of Major French Official Statements on Vietnam: August 29, 1963-February 21, 1966*. New York, 1966.

———. *Excerpts of Major French Official Statements on Vietnam: July 2, 1966-February 28, 1968*. New York, 1968.

———. *Foreign Affairs.* Selected Numbers, 1963-1968. New York.

———. *France and Vietnam Major French Statements August 1963-December 1973*. New York, 1974.

———. *French Affairs.* Selected Numbers, 1963-1968. New York.

———. *Major Addresses, Statements and Press Conferences of General Charles de Gaulle: May 19, 1958-January 31, 1964*. New York, 1964.

———. *Major Addresses, Statements and Press Conferences of General Charles de Gaulle: March 17, 1964-May 16, 1967*. New York, 1967.

———. *Press Releases.* Selected Numbers, 1963-1970.

———. *Speeches and Press Conferences.* Selected Numbers, 1963-1968. New York.

_____. *Statements of M. Maurice Couve de Murville, 1958-1966*. New York, 1966.
John F. Kennedy Library. *National Security Council Files*.
_____. *President's Office Files*.
_____. *Oral History Interviews*.
U.S. Congress. Senate Committee on Government Operations. *Hearings on the Atlantic Alliance* (Part 7). 89th Congress, 2nd Session, 1966.
_____. House Committee on Armed Services. *United States-Vietnam Relations 1945-1967; Study prepared by Department of Defense* (The Pentagon Papers). 12 vols. Washington, D.C.: U.S. Government Printing Office, 1971.
U.S. Senate. Committee on Foreign Relations. *Hearings on Causes, Origins and Lessons of Vietnam War, May 9, 10, 11, 1972*. Washington, D.C.: U.S. Government Printing Office, 1972.

BOOKS AND MONOGRAPHS

Aron, Raymond. *De Gaulle, Israel et Les Juifs*. Paris: Plon, 1968.
_____. *France Steadfast and Changing: The Fourth to The Fifth Republic*. Cambridge, Mass.: Harvard University Press, 1960.
_____. *The Great Debate: Theories of Nuclear Strategy*. New York: Anchor Books, 1965.
_____. *Peace and War: A Theory of International Relations*. New York: Praeger, 1967.
Ashmore, Harry S., and Baggs, William C. *Mission to Hanoi*. New York: G. P. Putnam, 1968.
Balta, Paul, and Rulleau, Claudine. *La Politique Arabe de la France de de Gaulle à Pompidou*. Paris: Edition Sindbad, 1973.
Bidault, Georges. *Resistance*. New York: Praeger, 1967.
Bloch-Morhange, Jacques. *Le Gaullisme*. Paris: Plon, 1963.
Bohlen, Charles E. *Witness to History, 1929-1969*. New York: W. W. Norton, 1973.
Bonnefous, Edouard. *Les Milliards Qui S'Envolent: L'Aide française aux pays sous-développés*. Paris: Fayard, 1963.
Calleo, David. *The Atlantic Fantasy: The United States, NATO and Europe*. Baltimore: Johns Hopkins University Press, 1970.
Camps, Miriam. *Britain and the European Community, 1955-1963*. Princeton: Princeton University Press, 1964.
Carmoy, Guy de. *Les Politiques Etrangères de la France 1944-1966*. Paris: La Table Ronde, 1967.
Chaffard, Georges. *Les Deux guerres du Vietnam. De Valluy à Westmoreland*. Paris: La Table Ronde, 1969.
Chen, King. *Vietnam and China: 1938-1954*. Princeton: Princeton University Press, 1969.
Chesneaux, Jean. *Le Vietnam*. Paris: F. Maspero, 1968.
_____; Boudarel, Georges; and Hemery, Daniel. eds. *Tradition et revolution au Vietnam*. Paris: Anthropos, 1971.
Cooper, Chester L. *Lost Crusade: America in Vietnam*. New York: Dodd, Mead, 1970.

Couve de Murville, Maurice. *Une Politique Etrangère, 1958-1969.* Paris: Plon, 1971.

De Gaulle, Charles. *The Army of the Future.* Philadelphia: J. B. Lippincott Co., 1941.

_____. *The War Memoirs of Charles de Gaulle.* 3 vols. New York: Simon and Schuster, 1955, 1959, 1960.

_____. *Discours et Messages.* Paris: Plon, 1970.

_____. *Le fil de l'epée.* Paris: Berger-Lebrault, 1944.

_____. *Memoirs d'Espoir: Le renouveau 1955-1962; L'Effort 1962-.* Paris: Librairie Plon, 1970, 1971.

Devillers, Philippe. *The Struggle for The Unification of Vietnam.* London: Ilford House, 1962.

_____, and Lacouture, Jean. *End of a War: Indochina, 1954.* New York: Praeger, 1969.

Dommen, Arthur J. *Conflict in Laos, The Politics of Neutralization.* New York: Praeger, 1964.

Eden, Anthony. *Towards Peace in Indochina.* London: Oxford University Press, 1966.

Ely, Paul. *Memoires-Indochine dans la tourmente.* Paris: Plon, 1964.

Fall, Bernard. *Anatomy of a Crisis: The Laotian Crisis of 1960-1961.* New York: Doubleday, 1969.

_____. *Hell in a Very Small Place.* Philadelphia: J. B. Lippincott Co., 1967.

_____. *Last Reflections on a War.* Garden City: Doubleday, 1967.

_____. *Street without Joy.* 3rd ed. revised. Harrisburg, Pa.: Telegraphic Press, 1961.

_____. *Viet-Nam Witness 1953-1966.* London: Pall Mall Press, 1966.

Fedder, Edwin H. *NATO: The Dynamics of Alliance in the Post-War World.* New York: Dodd, Mead, 1973.

Fishel, Wesley R. ed. *Vietnam: Anatomy of a Conflict.* Itasca, Ill.: F. E. Peacock Publications, 1968.

Galante, Pierre. *Le Général.* Paris: Presses de la Cité, 1968.

Gavin, James M. *Crisis Now.* New York: Random House, 1968.

Gettleman, Marvin E. ed. 2nd ed. *Vietnam: History, Documents and Opinions on a Major World Crisis.* New York: New American Library, 1970.

Gilpin, Robert. *United States Power and the Multinational Corporation.* New York: Basic Books, 1975.

Gordon, David C. *The Passing of French Algeria.* London: Oxford University Press, 1966.

Grosser, Alfred. *La Politique extérieure de la Ve république.* Paris: Editions du Seuil, 1965.

_____. *La Politique extérieure française: continuités et discontinuités.* Paris: Fondation Nationale des Sciences Politique, 1970.

Gurtov, Melvin. *The First Vietnam Crisis: Chinese Communist Strategy and United States Involvement 1953-1954.* New York: Columbia University Press, 1967.

Halberstam, David. *The Best and the Brightest.* New York: Random House, 1969.

Halpern, A. M. ed. *Policies Toward China: Views from Six Continents.* New York: McGraw-Hill, 1965.

Hammer, Ellen J. *The Struggle for Indochina*. Stanford, Calif.: Stanford University Press, 1954.

Hess, John L. *The Case for de Gaulle*. New York: William Morrow and Co., 1968.

Hilsman, Roger. *To Move a Nation*. New York: Doubleday, 1967.

Hinton, Harold. *China's Turbulent Quest*. New York: Macmillan, 1970.

——. *Communist China in World Politics*. Boston: Houghton-Mifflin Co., 1966.

Hoffman, Stanley. *Decline or Renewal? France Since the 1930s*. New York: Viking Press, 1974.

——. *Gulliver's Troubles*. New York: McGraw-Hill, 1968.

—— ed. *In Search of France*. Cambridge, Mass.: Harvard University Press, 1963.

Hoopes, Townsend. *The Limits of Intervention*. New York: McKay, 1970.

Hsiao, Gene T. ed. *The Role of External Powers in Indochina*. Edwardsville, Ill.: Southern Illinois University, 1973.

Hull, Cordell. *Memoirs*. New York: Macmillan, 1948.

Humbaraci, Arslan. *Algeria: A Revolution That Failed; A Political History Since 1954*. New York: Praeger, 1966.

Irving, R.E.M. *The First Indochina War*. London: Crown Helm, 1975.

Johnson, Lyndon B. *The Vantage Point: Perspectives of the Presidency, 1963-1969*. New York: Holt, Rinehart and Winston, 1971.

Kelly, George Armstrong. *Lost Soldiers, The French Army and Empire in Crisis*. Cambridge, Mass.: M. I. T. Press, 1965.

Kissinger, Henry A. *The Troubled Partnership: A Re-appraisal of the Atlantic Alliance*. New York: McGraw-Hill, 1965.

Kohl, Wilfrid L. *French Nuclear Diplomacy*. Princeton: Princeton University Press, 1971.

Kolodiej, Edward A. *French International Policy Under de Gaulle and Pompidou: The Politics of Grandeur*. Ithaca, N.Y.: Cornell University Press, 1974.

Kraslow, David, and Loory, Stuart H. *The Secret Search for Peace in Vietnam*. New York: Vintage Books, 1968.

Kulski, Wladyslaw W. *De Gaulle and the World: The Foreign Policy of the Fifth French Republic*. Syracuse, N.Y.: Syracuse University Press, 1966.

Lacouture, Jean. *Citations du President de Gaulle*. Paris: Editions du Seuil, 1968.

——. *De Gaulle*. New York: Avon Books, 1968.

——. *Ho Chi Minh*. New York: Vintage Books, 1970.

——. *Vietnam: Between Two Truces*. New York: Vintage Books, 1966.

La Gorce, Paul Marie de. *De Gaulle entre deux mondes: Une vie et une époque*. Paris: Fayard, 1964.

——. *La France contre les empires*. Paris: B. Grasset, 1969.

Lancaster, Donald. *The Emancipation of French Indochina*. London: Oxford University Press, 1961.

Larteguy, Jean. *Un Million de dollars*. Paris: R. Solar, 1965.

——. *Voyage au bont de la guerre*. Paris: Presses de la Cité, 1971.

Ligot, Maurice. *Les accords de cooperation entre la France et les Etats Africains et malgache d'expression français*. Paris: Documentation Française, 1964.

Liska, George. *Imperial America*. Baltimore: Johns Hopkins University Press, 1967.

_____. *Nations in Alliance.* Baltimore: Johns Hopkins University Press, 1962.

Lusignan, Guy de. *French-Speaking Africa Since Independence.* New York: Praeger, 1969.

Macridis, Roy C. ed. *De Gaulle, Implacable Ally.* New York: Harper and Row, 1966.

Mallet, Serge. *Le Gaullisme et la Gauche.* Paris: Editions du Seuil, 1965.

Manac'h, Etienne. *Memoires d'Extreme Asie.* Paris: Fayard, 1977.

Maneli, Mieczyslaw. *War of the Vanquished.* New York: Harper and Row, 1971.

Massip, Roger. *De Gaulle et l'Europe.* Paris: Flammarion, 1963.

Moch, Jules. *Rencontres avec de Gaulle.* Paris: Plon, 1971.

Modelski, George. *International Conference on the Settlement of the Laotian Question, 1961-62.* Canberra: Australian National University, Department of International Relations, 1962.

Morse, Edward L. *Foreign Policy and Interdependence in Gaullist France.* Princeton: Princeton University Press, 1973.

Mus, Paul. *Ho Chi Minh, le Vietnam, l'Asie.* Paris: Editions du Seuil, 1971.

Newhouse, Edward. *De Gaulle and the Anglo-Saxons.* New York: Viking Press, 1969.

Nguyen, Kien. *Le Sud-Vietnam depuis Dien-Bien-Phu.* Paris: F. Maspero, 1963.

Passeron, André. *De Gaulle Parle; 1958-1962.* Paris: Fayard, 1962.

_____. *De Gaulle Parle; 1962-1966.* Paris: Fayard, 1966.

Pickles, Dorothy. *Algeria and France: From Colonialism to Cooperation.* New York: Praeger, 1963.

_____. *The Uneasy Entente: French Foreign Policy and Franco-British Misunderstandings.* London: Oxford University Press, 1966.

Pinder, Jean. *Europe Against de Gaulle.* New York: Praeger, 1963.

Poole, Peter A. *The United States and Indochina from FDR to Nixon.* Hinsdale, Ill.: The Dryden Press, 1973.

Porte, A. W. de. *De Gaulle's Foreign Policy, 1944-1946.* Cambridge, Mass.: Harvard University Press, 1968.

Porter, D. Gareth. *A Peace Denied: The United States, Vietnam, and the Paris Agreement.* Bloomington: Indiana University Press, 1976.

Randle, Robert. *Geneva 1954: The Settlement of the Indochinese War.* Princeton: Princeton University Press, 1969.

Raskin, Marcus G., and Fall, Bernard B. eds. *The Viet-Nam Reader: Articles and Documents on American Foreign Policy and the Vietnam Crisis.* New York: Vintage Books, 1967.

Reynaud, Paul. *La Politique étrangère du gaullisme.* Paris: Julliard, 1964.

Robinson, Frank M., and Kemp, Earl. *Report of the U.S. Senate Hearings: The Truth about Vietnam.* San Diego, Calif.: Greenleaf Classics Inc., 1966.

Roy, Jules. *The Battle of Dienbienphu.* New York: Harper and Row, 1963.

Saint Robert, Philippe de. *Le Jeu de la France en Mediterrané, 1970.* Paris: Julliard, 1967.

Sainteny, Jean. *Histoire d'une paix manquée.* Paris: Amyot Dumont, 1953.

_____. *Ho Chi Minh and His Vietnam; A Personal Memoir.* Chicago: Cowles, 1972.

Scheer, Robert. *How the United States Got Involved in Vietnam.* Santa Barbara, Calif.: Center for the Study of Democratic Institutions, 1965.

Scheinman, Lawrence. *Atomic Energy Policy in France Under the Fourth Republic.* Princeton: Princeton University Press, 1965.

Schoenbrun, David. *The Three Lives of Charles de Gaulle.* New York: Atheneum, 1966.

Schurmann, Franz; Scott, Peter Dale; and Zelnik, Reginald. *The Politics of Escalation in Vietnam.* Greenwich, Conn.: Fawcett, 1966.

Serfaty, Simon. *France, De Gaulle and Europe.* Baltimore: Johns Hopkins University Press, 1968.

Shaplen, Robert. *The Lost Revolution.* New York: Harper and Row, 1965.

Sulzberger, C. L. *The Last of the Giants.* New York: Macmillan, 1970.

Tran-Minh Tiet. *Les Relations américano-vietnamiennes de Kennedy à Nixon.* 3 vols. Paris: Nouvelles editions latines, 1972.

Wajsman, Patrick, and René-François Teissedre, eds. *Nos Politiciens face au conflict israélo-arabe.* Paris: Fayard, 1969.

Weinstein, Franklin B. *Vietnam's Unheld Elections: The Failure to Carry Out the 1956 Reunification Elections and the Effect on Hanoi's Present Outlook.* Ithaca, N.Y.: Cornell University Southeast Asia Program, Data Paper #60.

Werth, Alexander. *De Gaulle: A Political Biography.* New York: Simon and Schuster, 1966.

Williams, Philip M. *The French Parliament.* New York: Praeger, 1968.

———. *Crisis and Compromise: Politics in the Fourth Republic.* Garden City: Doubleday, 1966.

Willis, F. Roy. *France, Germany and the New Europe.* Stanford, Calif.: Stanford University Press, 1965.

———. ed. *De Gaulle: Anachronism, Realist or Prophet?* New York: Holt, Rinehart and Winston, 1967.

Wilson, Harold. *Personal Record: The Labour Government 1964-1970.* Boston: Little, Brown, 1971.

ARTICLES AND PERIODICALS

Ailleret, Charles Louis. "Defense in All Directions," *Atlantic Community Quarterly,* 4, no. 1 (Spring 1968), 17-25. (Reprinted from *Revue de Défense Nationale,* December 1967.)

Alexander, Pierre. "Francophonie: The French and Africa," *Journal of Contemporary History,* 4 (January 1969), pp. 117-125.

Aron, Raymond. "From Independence to Neutrality," *Atlantic Community Quarterly,* 6, no. 2 (Summer 1968), 267-269. (Reprinted from *Le Figaro,* February 22, 1968.)

———. "Tour de Valse," *Le Figaro,* March 1, 1965, pp. 1, 32.

Beaufre, André. "Commentaires sur une conception de la Stratégie," *Revue de Défense Nationale,* 19 (December 1963), pp. 1802-1810.

Bernetel, D. "France-Afrique: rien n'a change," *Jeune Afrique,* 576 (January 22, 1972), pp. 12-13.

Britsch, Jacques. "Le Destin de la peninsule indochinoise," *Revue de Défense Nationale*, 19, no. 12 (December 1963), pp. 1823-1835.

_____. "Les Intérêts Français dans la péninsule indochinoise," *Revue de Défense Nationale*, 20, no. 5 (May 1964), pp. 864-880.

Caldwell, Dan. "Détente in Historical Perspective," *International Studies Notes*, 3, no. 4 (Winter 1976), pp. 17-20.

Carmoy, Guy de. "France and the Atlantic Community," *Current History*, 58 (May 1970), pp. 269-275.

_____. "The Last Year of de Gaulle's Foreign Policy," *International Affairs* (July 1969), pp. 424-435.

Chauvel, Jean. "L'affaire du Vietnam au printemps 1965," *Revue de Défense Nationale*, 21 (August-September 1965), pp. 1328-1335.

_____. "La Voie Difficile d'une paix au Vietnam," *Le Figaro*, February 10, 1966, pp. 1, 4.

_____. "Le Sud-Est asiatique et la politique francaise," *Revue de deux mondes*, 8 (April 15, 1965), pp. 481-493.

_____. "Les Accords sur le Vietnam," *Politique Etrangère* (1973), no. 1, pp. 13-27.

_____. "Les Chances de paix au Vietnam," *Le Figaro*, January 3, 1966, pp. 1, 4.

Couve de Murville, Maurice. "French Foreign Policy: Our Position," *Vital Speeches*, 30 (November 15, 1963), p. 74.

Daniel, Jean. "Le myth Gaulliste dans le 'Tiers Monde'," *Le Monde*, February 5, 1964, pp. 1-2.

Debré, Michel. "France's Global Strategy," *Foreign Affairs*, 49 (April 1971), pp. 395-406.

"De Gaulle's Eastern Europe," *East Europe*, 14 (January 1965), pp. 13-15.

Devillers, Philippe. "French Policy and the Second Vietnam War," *World Today*, 23, no. 6 (June 1962), pp. 249-261.

_____. "The Paris Negotiations on Vietnam," *The World Today*, 25, no. 8 (August 1969), pp. 339-350.

_____. "Vietnam: la fin des chimères?" *Politique aujourd'hui*, February 2, 1969, pp. 28-32.

Devinat, Paul. "Un Renouveau Franco-Vietnamien est-il possible?" *Politique Etrangère*, 21, no. 4 (July-August 1956), pp. 427-442.

Dulles, John Foster. "The Threat of Red China," *Department of State Bulletin*, 30 (April 12, 1954), p. 541.

Duncanson, Dennis J. "Vietnam and Foreign Powers," *International Affairs*, 45, no. 3 (July 1969), pp. 413-423.

Duroselle, Jean-Baptiste. "The Crisis in French Foreign Policy," *Review of Politics*, 16 (October 1954), pp. 412-437.

Duverger, Maurice. "Le Silence de l'Europe," *Le Monde*, February 15, 1968, pp. 1-3.

Evenou (Vice Admiral d'escadre). "L'O.T.A.S.E. en 1963," *Revue de Défense Nationale*, 19 (July 1963), pp. 1098-1109.

Fall, Bernard B. "La Politique américaine au Vietnam," *Politique Etrangère*, 20, no. 3 (June-July 1955), pp. 299-322.

_____. "Vietnam: The Agonizing Reappraisal," *Current History*, 48 (February 1965), pp. 95-102.

_____. "What de Gaulle Actually Said about Vietnam," *Reporter*, 29 (October 24, 1963), pp. 39-41.

Finney, John. "U.S. Urged to Reveal Note to French on Peace Talks," *New York Times*, September 9, 1966, p. 1.

Fontaine, André. "Beaucoup de Questions et Quelques Résponses," *Le Monde*, January 19-20, 1964, pp. 1-2; January 21, 1964, p. 2; January 22, 1964, p. 2 (three-part series).

_____. "Depasser L'Endiquement," *Le Monde*, February 11, 1965, pp. 1-3.

_____. "Histoire des Deux Chines," *Le Monde*, January 28, 1964, p. 2; January 29, 1964, p. 3; January 30, 1964, p. 2 (three-part series).

_____. "L'Europe et l'Asie," *Le Monde*, March 9, 1965, pp. 1-2.

Gallois, Pierre M. "Faux paradoxes et verités paradoxales," *Politique Etrangère*, 28 (1963), pp. 317-329.

_____. "La Nouvelle Politique Extérieure des Etats-Unis et la Securité de l'Europe," *Revue de Défense Nationale*, 19 (April 1963), pp. 566-594.

_____. "La Nouvelle Stratégie Americaine et ses contradictions," *Politique Etrangère*, 26, no. 4 (1961), pp. 320-326.

_____. "Pierrelatte à ses raisons," *Politique Etrangère*, 27, no. 5 (1962), 453-461.

Garder, Michel. "Le jeu de la dissuasion dans la crise au Vietnam," *Revue de Defense Nationale*, 21, no. 5 (May 1965), pp. 706-712.

Grosser, Alfred. "Divergences Franco-Allemandes," *Revue de Défense Nationale*, 21, no. 1 (January 1965), pp. 13-20.

_____. "La Comparison Algerienne," *Le Monde*, September 4-5, 1966, pp. 1-2.

Guillain, Robert. "Une Seule Chine," *Le Monde*, February 1, 1964, pp. 1-2.

Halberstam, David. "French Discount Letter by Rusk," *New York Times*, September 11, 1966, p. 3.

Hammer, Ellen J. "The Struggle for Indochina Continues," *Pacific Spectator*, 9, supplement (Summer 1955), pp. 1-4.

Hippolyte, Mirlande. "Regroupings in Francophone Africa," *Africa Quarterly*, 8, no. 4 (January-March 1969), pp. 343-358.

Hoffher, René. "L'aide de la France aux pays en voie de développement," *Revue de Défense Nationale*, 21, no. 5 (May 1965), pp. 730-740.

Hoffmann, Stanley. "Minimum Feasible Misunderstanding; America and France," *New Republic*, 160 (April 5, 1969), 17-21, and 160 (April 12, 1969), pp. 20-23.

_____. "De Gaulle's Legacy to Pompidou," *New Republic* 161 (July 12, 1969), pp. 19-21, and 161 (July 26, 1969), pp. 21-25.

_____. "The Will to Grandeur: de Gaulle as Political Artist," *Daedalus* (Summer 1968), pp. 829-887.

Irvine, Keith. "Franczone Africa," *Current History*, 56, no. 333 (May 1969), pp. 282-285.

Joyaux, François. "La Conférence de Manille, 24-25 October 1966," *Politique Etrangère*, 31, nos. 5-6 (1966), pp. 534-541.

_____. "Perspectives de paix au Viet-Nam," *Revue de Défense Nationale* (October 1968), pp. 1503-1510.

Kahin, George McT. "The Pentagon Papers: A Critical Evaluation," *American Political Science Review* 69, no. 2 (June 1975), pp. 675-684.

Kerven, Daniel (pseudonym). "Esquisse sur la politique asiatique de la France," *France-Asie/Asia*, 185 (Spring 1966), pp. 286-302.

Kissinger, Henry A. "Coalition Diplomacy in a Nuclear Age," *Foreign Affairs*, 42, no. 4 (1964), pp. 525-545.

Kolodziej, Edward A. "France and the Atlantic Alliance: Alliance with a De-Aligning Power," *Polity* (1970), pp. 242-266.

————. "Revolt and Revisionism in the Gaullist Global Vision," *Journal of Politics*, 33 (May 1971), pp. 448-477.

Lacouture, Jean. "Des à-peu-près pour le passé et une idée pour l'avenir," *Le Monde*, July 25, 1964, pp. 1-3.

————. "Guerre Indochinoise: 1946-1954," *Le Monde*, November 19, 1966, pp. 1-4; November 20-21, 1966, p. 2 (two-part series).

————. "L'Opinion Française et la Second Guerre du Vietnam," *Le Monde*, December 13, 1966, pp. 1-3.

————. "Neuf Ans Après," *Le Monde*, August 31, 1963, pp. 1-2.

————. "Retour à l'Indochine," *Le Monde*, May 26, 1964, pp. 1-2.

La Feber, Walter. "Roosevelt, Churchill, and Indochina: 1942-45," *American Historical Review* 80 (December 1975), pp. 1277-1295.

L'Annee Politique. Selected Numbers.

Le Figaro. (1963-1977).

Le Gorgne, Julien. "Dix Ans de Politique Américaine au Vietnam," *Revue de Défense Nationale*, 20, no. 10 (October 1964), pp. 1613-1631.

Le Monde (1963-1977).

Lenart, E. R. "End Game in Paris," *Far East Economic Revue*, 65 (August 7, 1969), pp. 370-372.

Levergne, B. "Libres Réflexions sur les mérites et les déficiences de la politique extérieure de la Ve rép à propos du livre très remarquable de M. Couve de Murville," *Année politique et economique*, 44 (December 1971), pp. 389-410.

"Le Vietnam entre la guerre et la paix," *Tiers-Monde*, 11, nos. 42-43 (April-September 1970), pp. 261-632.

Luc, Jean Claude. "Prospects of Forming a Francophone Community," *Africa Quarterly*, 9, no. 2 (July-September 1969), pp. 113-130.

Marchand, Jean. "La Guerre d'Indochine," *Revue de Défense Nationale*, 21, no. 10 (October 1968), pp. 1529-1541.

Massip, Roger. "Pourquoi," *Le Figaro*, February 2, 1966, p. 4.

Masson, Claude. "Les Aspects economiques de la francophonie," *Etudes internationales* (Quebec) 1, no. 3 (September 1970), pp. 26-44.

Maulnier, Theirry. "Nouvelle Lettre aux Americains," *Le Figaro*, April 9, 1965, pp. 1, 18.

Mende, Tibor. "La Chine en quete d'un contexte asiatique," *Revue de Défense Nationale*, 19 (October 1963), pp. 1447-1465.

Mendel, Wolf. "After de Gaulle: Continuity and Change in French Foreign Policy," *World Today*, 27 (January 1971), pp. 8-17.

_____. "The Background of French Nuclear Policy," *International Affairs* (London), 41 (January 1965), pp. 22-36.

Messmer, Pierre. "Notre Politique Militaire," *Revue de Défense Nationale* (May 1963), pp. 745-761.

Micaud, Charles A. "Gaullism After de Gaulle," *Orbis*, 14, no. 3 (Fall 1970), pp. 657-672.

Moch, Jules and Gallois, Pierre. "Les Conséquences Stratégiques et Politiques des Armes Nouvelles," *Politique Étrangère*, 23, no. 2 (1958), pp. 149-167 and 168-180, respectively.

Mooney, Richard E. "Hanoi Envoy Hints End to Bombing Could Spur Talks," *New York Times*, January 6, 1967, p. 1.

Nemo (General). "Au Vietnam, de la théorie à la practique," *Revue de Défense Nationale*, 21 (June 1965), pp. 1022-1028.

_____. "La guerre civile du Viet Nam," *Revue de Défense Nationale*, 21 (November 1965), pp. 1743-1751.

Newhouse, J. "Revisiting Laos: de Gaulle and the Three Princes," *Interplay* (March 1970), pp. 50-54.

New York Times. (1963-1973).

Oakeshott, Robert. "What France Is Up To: Speculation in the French Capital about President de Gaulle's Press Conference on January 31 (1964) and Its Implications for Asia," *Far Eastern Economic Review*, 43 (February 27, 1964), pp. 459-461.

Pelissier, Roger. "Trois Siècles de Relations Franco-Chinoises," *Le Monde*, January 28, 1964, pp. 1-3; January 29, 1964, p. 4.

Pepy, Daniel. "France's Relations with Africa," *African Affairs*, 69, no. 275 (April 1970), pp. 155-162.

Politique Étrangère. Selected Numbers.

Porter, D. Gareth. "Vietnam: Politics of the Paris Agreement," *Current History*, 65 (December 1973), pp. 247-251.

Reston, James. "Washington: The Private Maneuvers on Vietnam," *New York Times*, September 9, 1966, p. 44.

Revue de Défense Nationale. Selected numbers.

Rouanet, Pierre. "Hopeless War in Vietnam: de Gaulle's Views," *New Statesman*, 69 (March 5, 1965), p. 348.

Rouillon F. "La politique française au Moyen-Orient et ses relations avec la politique américaine," *Politique Étrangère*, 36 (1971), pp. 647-655.

Rouleau, Eric. "French Policy in the Middle East," *World Today*, 24, no. 5 (May 1968), pp. 209-218.

Roustide, Pierre. "La France et l'OTAN," *Revue de Défense Nationale*, 20 (May 1964), pp. 802-815.

Sandrin, Christian. "Les 'Hameaux Stratégiques' au Sud-Vietnam," *Revue de Défense Nationale*, 19 (December 1963), pp. 1836-1846.

Servoise, René. "La Cooperation avec l'Afrique nouvelle," *Politique Étrangère*, 26 (1961), pp. 124-138.

Soustelle, Jacques. "De Gaulle and China: An Analysis," *New Leader*, 40 (April 13, 1964), pp. 14-16.

Sondages: revue française de l'opinion publique. 1965-1972.

Steele, Ronald. "Where France and China Agree: Common Frustrations, Common Maneuvers," *New Leader*, 47 (June 8, 1964), pp. 19-22.

St. John, Peter. "Independent Algeria from Ben Bella to Boumedienne," *World Today*, 24, no. 8 (August 1968), pp. 340-344.

St. Marc, Phillippe. "Les Grands Problèmes de la construction européenne," *Revue de Défense Nationale*, 21, no. 5 (May 1965), pp. 753-765.

Sullivan, Marianna P. "France and the Vietnam Peace Settlement," *Political Science Quarterly*, 89, no. 2 (June 1974), pp. 305-324.

Sulzberger, C. L. "De Gaulle and the United States," *Atlantic Community Quarterly*, 6, no. 1 (Spring 1968), 26-28. (Reprinted from the *New York Times*, January 28, 1968.)

Szulc, Tad. "Behind the Vietnam Cease-Fire Agreement," *Foreign Policy*, no. 15 (Summer 1974), pp. 21-70.

Theysset E. "Presence française in asie du sud-est," *Cooperation Technique*, 60 (March-April 1970), pp. 16-20.

"Toward a Greater French Community," *Current History*, 54 (March 1968), pp. 143-150.

Valluy, (General). "Réflexions sur le déterrent," *Revue de Défense Nationale*, 19, no. 6 (June 1963), pp. 925-937.

Van Alstyne, Richard. "The Vietnam War in Historical Perspective," *Current History*, 65 (December 1973), pp. 241-246.

Veilly, M. "L'enjeu des négociations sur le Viet-Nam," *Revue de Défense Nationale* (January 1969), pp. 44-54.

Vernant, Jacques. "Après le voyage presidentiel au Mexique," *Revue de Défense Nationale*, 20, no. 5 (May 1964), pp. 880-886.

———. "La Crise du Vietnam et le dilemme nucléaire," *Revue de Défense Nationale*, 22, no. 1 (January 1966), pp. 132-136.

———. "La Politique Extérieure de la France," *Revue de Défense Nationale*, 19 (July 1963), pp. 1196-1202, 19 (August 1963), pp. 1391-1396, and 19 (October 1963), pp. 1557-1561.

———. "Le général de Gaulle et la politique extérieure," *Politique Etrangère*, no. 6 (Summer 1960), pp. 619-629.

———. "Les Etats-Unis et l'Asie du Sud-Est," *Revue de Défense Nationale*, 20 (April 1964), pp. 706-711.

———. "Sur le Vietnam et à propos de l'armament nucléaire," *Revue de Défense Nationale*, 23, no. 3 (March 1967), pp. 490-499.

"Waning Power of France in Vietnam," *World Today*, 12 (February 1956), pp. 50-58.

Washington Post (1965-1968).

UNPUBLISHED MATERIAL

Dean, John G. "Current French Policy toward Vietnam." Unpublished paper, delivered at Harvard University Center for International Affairs, March 1970.

Pulaski, Marianna T. "France's Political Role in the United Nations, 1958-1965." Master's thesis, University of Virginia, 1966.
Sullivan, Marianna P. "De Gaulle's Policy toward the Conflict in Vietnam, 1963-1969." Ph.D. dissertation, University of Virginia, 1971.

LIST OF RESPONDENTS FOR PERSONAL INTERVIEWS

George Aldrich, Legal Adviser, Department of State, Washington, D.C., November 1, 1973.

André Beaufre, Director, Office of Strategic Studies, Paris, France, June 30, 1972.

Charles E. Bohlen, former Ambassador to France, Washington, D.C. January 15, 1971.

Henri Bolle, Deputy Director, Section Asiatique, French Foreign Ministry, Paris, France, June 16, 1972.
Jean Brethes, formerly with the French Foreign Ministry, Paris, France, July 6, 1972.

Jean de Broglie, President, Commission des affairs Etrangères, Assemblé Nationale, Paris, France, July 21, 1972.

François Bujon de l'Estaing, French Embassy Official, Washington, D.C., September 7, 1972.

Wilfred Burchett, Journalist, Paris, France, July 17, 1972.

Patricia Byrne, United States Embassy Official, Paris, France, July 5, 1972.

Guy de Carmoy, Author, Paris, France, June 28, 1972.

Jean Chauvel, Ambassador (retired), Paris, France, June 20, 1972.

Peter Collins, Member, Vietnam Working Group, Washington, D.C., October 29, 1973.

Jacques de Cornoy, Journalist, Paris, France, June 29, 1972.

Maurice Couve de Murville, former Foreign Minister of France, Paris, France, July 6, 1972.

Nguyen Van Chi, Professor, Paris, France, July 7, 1972.

René Dabernat, Journalist, Paris, France, June 27, 1972.

Nguyen Trieu Dan, Press Spokesman, Delegation of the Republic of Vietnam to the Paris Peace Talks, Paris, France, June 16, 1972 and July 5, 1973.

Maurice Delarue, Journalist, Paris, France, July 5, 1973.

Phillippe Devillers, Author, Paris, France, June 23, 1972, July 24, 1972, and July 9, 1973.

André Fontaine, Editor, *Le Monde,* Paris, France, July 24, 1972.

Henri Froment-Meurice, Directeur d'Affaires Asie-Océanie, French Foreign Ministry, Paris, France, July 4, 1973.

Robert Frowich, State Department Official, Washington, D.C., November 1, 1973.

Henry Gininger, Journalist, Paris, France, June 20, 1972.

Serge de Gunsberg, Journalist, Paris, France, June 16, 1972.

Ellen Hammer, Author, Paris, France, July 4, 1972.

John L. Hess, Journalist, Paris, France, June 28, 1972.

Heywood Isham, State Department Official, Washington, D.C., October 31, 1973.

Elisabeth Kahn, Official of French Finance Ministry, Paris, France, July 9, 1973.

Nguyen Khai, Press Spokesman, Delegation of the Democratic Republic of Vietnam to France, Paris, July 24, 1972 and July 10, 1973.

Buu Kinh, Author, Paris, France, June 28, 1972.

Max Kraus, American Embassy Official, Paris, France, July 21, 1972.

Jean Lacouture, Author, Paris, France, July 5, 1972.

Paul Marie de la Gorce, Former Conseilleur Technique, Office of French Premier, Paris, France, July 11, 1972.

Roger Lalouette, Ambassador of France (retired), Fontainebleu, France, July 19, 1972.

David Lambertson, Press Spokesman, Delegation of the United States to the Paris Peace Talks, Paris, France, June 13, 1972.

Edith Lenart, Journalist, Paris, France, June 27, 1972.

Flora Lewis, Journalist, Paris, France, July 3, 1973.

Jean-Louis Lucet, Deputy Diplomatic Counselor, Office of the French President, Paris, France, June 30, 1972 and July 11, 1973.

Jean Lutton, Researcher, Centre National du Commerce Extérieur, Paris, France, June 29, 1973.

Henri Magné, Official of Union des Syndicats, Professionnels Indochinois, Paris, France, June 28, 1973.

Etienne Manac'h, French Ambassador to China, Paris, France, July 27, 1972.

Albert Mariau, Official of Section d'Amerique, French Foreign Ministry, Paris, France, June 21, 1972.

David Mason, Journalist, Paris, France, June 27, 1972.

Roger Massip, Author, Paris, France, August 23, 1972.

Jacques Mer, Official of French Foreign Ministry, Paris, France, July 9, 1972.

Marte Parent, Official of French Finance Ministry, Paris, France, July 5, 1973.

Marc Pratt, American Embassy Official, Paris, France, June 28, 1973.

William Porter, former Chief of Delegation of the United States to the Paris Peace Talks, Paris, France, July 21, 1972, and Washington, D.C., November 2, 1973.

Bernard Redmont, Journalist, Paris, France, July 10, 1972.

Robert Richmond, State Department Official, Washington, D.C., October 31, 1973.

Michel Rouganou, Deputy Director, Press Section, Office of the French President, Paris, France, June 22, 1972.

Eric Rouleau, Journalist, Paris, France, June 29, 1972.

Jean Sainteny, former French Delegate General to Hanoi, Paris, France, June 26, 1972, August 23, 1972, and July 6, 1973.

Le Marquis de Saint Legier de La Sausaye, former Diplomatic Adviser to General de Gaulle, Paris, France, July 11, 1973.

Ly Van Sau, Press Spokesman, Delegation of Provisional Revolutionary Government of South Vietnam to the Paris Peace Talks, Paris, France, July 3, 1973.

Savang, Cambodian Embassy Official, Paris, France, June 19, 1972.

Maurice Schumann, former French Foreign Minister, Paris, France, July 6, 1973.

William Stearman, Official of National Security Council, Washington, D.C., October 31, 1973.

Paul Stehlin, Member of Assemblé Nationale, Paris, France, July 10, 1972.

Jacques Vernant, Author, Paris, France, June 29, 1972.

Cyrus R. Vance, Former Deputy Chief, United States Delegation to the Paris Peace Talks, New York, May 26, 1972.

Index

ABOUT THE AUTHOR

Marianna P. Sullivan is Associate Professor of Political Science at Trenton State College, Trenton, New Jersey. A specialist in French and American foreign policy, her articles have appeared in *Political Science Quarterly* and *The Role of External Powers in the Indochina Crisis,* edited by Gene T. Hsiao.